A WOMAN OF FAITH

A Faith-filled Memoir that shows how Christian beliefs transform struggles into moments of grace, offering Divine hope and strength through Life's challenges

Jennifer A Kyd

A WOMAN OF FAITH: A Faith – filled Memoir that shows how Christan beliefs transform struggles into moments of grace, offering Divine hope and strength through life's challenges.

Copyright © [2025] by [Jennifer A Kyd.]

All rights reserved. No portion of this book may be reproduced in any form or by any means without prior written permission from the author, except as permitted under Australian copyright law.

Printed in Australia.

Artwork by Anne Pannaye

All Scripture quotations are taken from The Holy Bible Revised Standard Version – Second Catholic Edition.

ISBN: 978-1-7644277-0-8

First Edition: 2025

Contents

Image of White Garment	V
Vision on the bus in the Holy Land	VI
FOREWORD	VII
1. Introduction	1
2. The Divine Nudge: A Calling I Couldn't Ignore	5
3. A Life Shaped by Faith and Loss	9
4. Prayers, Loss, and Grace in a New Home	17
5. The Healing Power of Faith	23
6. Faith in the Face of Fear	29
7. The Diagnosis That Shook Us Both	39
8. Touching the Heart of the Holy Land	43
9. Prayers, Patience, and Unexpected Blessings	51
10. When Few Gather, God Still Moves	55
11. Parousia and the Message I Couldn't Ignore	61
12. Unexpected Guests and God's Perfect Plan	65
13. The Power of Prayer in God's Perfect Plan	69

14.	How God's Whisper Became a Book	77
15.	A stranger's card and a silent message	87
16.	When God's Plan Unfolds in Mysterious Ways	93
17.	A Divine Revelation Beyond Physical Bread	99
18.	The 15-Year Prayer That Changed Everything	107
19.	Learning to Abide in Love	115
20.	The Message Behind Parousia	123
21.	Why Praying for Priests is Vital for the Church	125
22.	The Dream That Urged Me to Pray for the World's Redemption	129
23.	A Call to Honor the Sacredness of God's Dwelling	137
24.	Called to Be a Witness	141
25.	Seeing God's Presence in Every Living Creature	145
26.	A Journey of Prayer and Miracles for a Little Life	147
CONCLUSION		155
ACKNOWLEDGEMENTS		159
ENDNOTES		161
THANK YOU		163

Image of White Garment

ALL THINGS ARE POSSIBLE TO HIM
WHO BELIEVES MK 9:23
COURTESY OF DIVINE RETREAT CENTRE

Vision on the Bus in the Holy Land

FOREWORD

Jenny is a woman of Faith, and I have known her for more than six years as a volunteer for God's work. She visited me often for spiritual guidance, asking if God called her to write this awe-inspiring book. We prayed, and I felt that it would help develop faith. The one who is loved receives and then gives the same love to all others.

The work is Christian and written in the light of the meaning of the Gospel of Jesus Christ, with its many facets that extend into all aspects of life. The book aptly describes inspirational insights that she had received from the Holy Spirit. It deals with areas where everyone should be informed to be thoughtful members of their religious communities. It answers many doubts and will surely increase the faith of many.

Strength, wisdom, awareness, and reasoning are required for change, and prayer can be a powerful weapon against the forces of evil. The transformative power of faith is beautifully encapsulated in (Hebrews 1:11-6): "But without faith, it is impossible to please Him, for he who comes to God must believe that He is and that He is a rewarder of those who diligently seek Him." This verse is a beacon of hope, empowering us to face life's challenges with unwavering faith.

I thank God for providing answers to many questions through this book. Jenny's thoughts, beautifully articulated in this book, have the potential to make a profound difference in the lives of others. As we consciously attune ourselves to recognise that the Lord is speaking to us in events and through persons, we can't help but appreciate the book's contribution to our Christian community.

I thank Jenny for delving into the intricacies of such a complex but essential aspect of life and relationships. I appreciate Ms Jenny's work, which will inspire the children of God and gradually increase the faith of millions. Beyond reasoning is faith; the book has been written responsibly and with gratitude.

Fr. Roni George VC, Director,

Divine Retreat Centre,

2250

(Since September 2024, Fr. Roni has been the director of the Divine Retreat Centre in Toronto.)

John 2:5

I have known Jenny since my days at the Divine Retreat Centre, when it first started on Lutana Road. She initially was just an acquaintance I met as a retreatant. But the more often I met her at the retreats, the more I got to know a person who desires to live that Marian exhortation, "Do whatever He asks you to do."

Driving about one and a half hours from Penrith to attend all the retreats at the centre was never easy. A woman of few words but a great passion for being formed by the Spirit helped her soak in all the Word she could listen to.

I believe that has helped her to be led by the Spirit to write this book. Her discipleship journey was moulded by her faithfulness to the Lord and her commitment to let His plans be fulfilled in her.

May this book inspire many, as Jenny was inspired and led by the Holy Spirit.

Fr Michael Payyapilly, VC Director,
Divine Retreat Centre, Colombo

Artist's Profile

I invited the artist who painted the vision I had in the Holy Land to share her story about her experience and the emotions she encountered while trying to paint the vision for me. I know the difficulties she went through and the wonderful experience she encountered when she did a practice run of the face of Jesus. When I asked her, I knew it would be challenging to paint an image someone else has in their head and not to have seen it. I believed the Lord chose her, and she would complete the vision shown to me.

This is her story

This project has been my most significant artistic challenge so far. Jenny, the author of these writings, asked me to do this special painting for her several years ago. It has been a work in progress and a complete standstill for some time.

Painting and drawing have been my passions since I was very young. I have attended numerous art classes and tutorials, even from several well-known Australian artists, and only took an advanced diploma course in painting. Drawing techniques were also taught at the local TAFE.

I have spent many hours preparing for this painting. I have never drawn or even attempted to draw the face of Jesus, and did not think I could. However, one day, while staying with friends and alone in their home, I was prompted to try. This was my first attempt, and with each stroke I made, I felt the prompting of the Holy Ghost. It became so overwhelming that I began to cry; I couldn't stop crying and had to stop drawing. I am grateful for this opportunity, which has stretched my Faith and ability to achieve this goal to the hilt. Thank you, Jenny, for giving me this opportunity and for having faith in me to complete this task.

Ann Pannaye

Chapter 1

Introduction

My dear brothers and sisters in Christ, be assured that a prayer has been offered for you as you read this book.

It has taken me many years to complete this book, as I had to pray and discern if this was what God was asking of me. Sometimes, I doubted myself and wanted to give up, but the Spirit of the Lord gave me the courage to continue.

The contents of this book are based on facts, not fiction. One morning on my way to work, I had no idea that what was about to happen would change my life. It was the day the Spirit of the Lord made it very clear that I should write a book and gave me the title, 'A Woman of Faith.' I was shaking and trembling, my heart racing, and I felt afraid and confused about what had just occurred. That day, I prayed, asking God for validation on whether what I heard that morning was true, as it was the first time I had encountered such an experience.

"They said to each other, Did not our hearts burn within us while he talked to us on the road, while he opened to us the Scriptures?" (Luke 24:32).

I kept everything to myself for many years because I had no idea what to do or how to write a book. For years, the title troubled me; it was the letter A, as I felt it singled me out as an individual. Only towards the book's conclusion did I revert to the original title, believing it was what God wanted, coming directly from Him. From the time I was given this assignment, I felt a change within me. I practised humility, did not boast, and did not reveal to anyone what had happened.

I spent much time praying, trying to discern if this was what God asked of me. I became quiet and withdrawn, attempting to live according to the teachings of Christ. Another reason I kept everything to myself was that I didn't want anyone to doubt the power of God—that with Him, all things are possible. He is the Almighty One who created the heavens and the earth. I also didn't want to be surrounded by negativity, as many would have questioned whether God had truly asked this of me, which would have increased my insecurities and doubts at the time.

I decided to start writing down a few things, but I still wasn't sure if my actions were correct. After many years, the first person I confided in was Fr. Roni VC when I visited him for Spiritual Guidance. A few months later, I eventually spoke to Fr. Michael Belonio OSA, who was our parish priest during that period. I also confided in one other person.

This is where Faith played a tremendous role. After much prayer and discernment, I believed this was what God was asking of me, and I had to obey His Holy will. God was great, and I had to rely on Him throughout the writing of this book. The Holy Spirit inspired all visions; dreams are as they happened and are not exaggerated.

I pray for those who have never opened their Bibles, hoping that the Bible verses mentioned in this book inspire you to read the Bible, which is the Word of God, daily or as often as possible. God speaks to you through His Word, and the Word was made flesh. This book contains many Bible references, all inspired by God. Many were revealed through prayer and opening my Bible to find God's answers to my prayers.

As I write, the Lord's Spirit inspires me with a few words from a verse I must include. The verse is somewhat familiar, but I'm unsure of its author. I also need to find the chapter and verse numbers for reference. I had to Google to find the exact verse that God had given me.

I read the Bible, but that doesn't mean I know every chapter and verse. Many readings, such as the Book of Tobit, Jeremiah, Habakkuk, Malachi, and later Amos, surprised me because they aren't the books I usually read.

God answers my prayers and questions directly through the readings He guides me to. I am familiar with the New Testament and some of the Old Testament, having studied the first few books of the Old Testament. I also attended retreats where all talks were based on the Word of God.

To those of you who have lost hope and faith and are struggling to believe and trust in God, I pray that after you read this book, you will come to believe and trust that He can help you by transforming any situation from bad to good. All He asks is that you trust in Him and believe that whatever you ask in His name will be given to you, bringing a renewed sense of hope and inspiration into your life.

"So faith by itself, if it has no works, is dead." (James 2:17).

We need to act on what we believe to be true. It is easy to say I have Faith, but our actions must accompany it. I had Faith that God was calling me to author this book. If I chose to ignore this calling, my faith would be fruitless, as actions do not accompany it. This was not easy for me, but I put what God asked of me into action through prayer and supplication, empowering and motivating me to follow His guidance.

Chapter 2

The Divine Nudge: A Calling I Couldn't Ignore

"Am I a God at Hand, Says The Lord, And Not A God Of Afar Off? Can A Man Hide Himself In Secret Places So That I Cannot See Him? Says The Lord. Do I Not Fill Heaven And Earth? Says The Lord." (Jeremiah 23: 23-24).

At the start of 2024, I felt the Lord inspiring me to begin writing again and to finish the book. By the end of January and early February 2024, I sensed a profound presence of the Holy Spirit around me, which overwhelmed me and brought tears to my eyes. I had been feeling this way for a few weeks. On Saturday, 3rd February 2024, I rang Ann, the artist who is undertaking the task of painting the vision for me, to confide that I was experiencing a strong presence of the Spirit of the Lord and that He was revealing to me that I must complete the book, and this is the year to do it. We both agreed that we needed to work towards finishing the book and the painting before the end of the year.

From February 2nd to 4th, 2024, Fr. Antony Parankimalil VC conducted a weekend retreat at the Divine Retreat Centre in Somersby, NSW, each day from 9:00 a.m. to 4:00 p.m. Due to other commitments, I was unable to attend the retreat for the entire weekend, so I only attended on the last day. During Father Antony's talk, my name and a few others were called out, stating that the Lord was "touching our hearts."

Later, during Adoration, he said, "Someone is writing a Spiritual Book and must complete it." I was shocked, as I was not prepared to hear this message. When I heard this, I sat there frozen, saying nothing to anyone. I knew in my heart that God was validating what I had been feeling over the last few weeks, encouraging me to complete the book. God is always with us, guiding us on our spiritual journey.

For the rest of the afternoon, I tried to comprehend what had happened. After the retreat, most of us went for a Blessing. I told Fr Antony VC that I was authoring the Spiritual Book, so he prayed over me, gave me nine Bible verses to read, and said God would help me. One of the verses reads,

"I will not leave you desolate; I will come to you" (John 14:18). I cling to these words as they give me hope as God speaks to us through His Word.

These are the Scripture readings given to me by Fr. Antony.

John 14:18

Psalm 16:4

1 Peter 1:18-19

Psalm 86: 4

1 Corinthians 10:13

Revelation 21: 3- 6

Romans 8:18

Isaiah 58:11-12

Philippians 4:13

God is so great that He knows everything that happens in our lives, and we cannot run or hide from him. Everything we do or say, in word, thought, deed, or secret, which is not pleasing to God, believe that He knows and sees everything we do.

"Am I a God at hand, says the Lord, and not a God of afar off? Can a man hide himself in secret places so that I cannot see him? says the Lord. Do I not fill heaven and earth? says the Lord." (Jeremiah 23: 23-24).

When I returned home that evening, I was still amazed by what had occurred during the Retreat. The fact that I had felt the Spirit of the Lord so strongly in the weeks leading up to the Retreat made it feel surreal when I heard Fr. Antony say, "Someone is writing a Spiritual Book and must complete it." I began to realise that God knows everything. He understands what is in our hearts. I was experiencing mixed emotions and felt anxious and afraid about whether I could finish the book within the timeframe God had given me. I had hit a roadblock and questioned whether God was calling me to author this book. I doubted myself and my ability to complete it.

This is where my faith is put to the test. Do I believe God will help me finish this book within the timeframe He has set? Do I completely trust God to take control and obey His will? Do I believe God will not leave me desolate and will come to me when I need Him? As a Christian, I have to say yes. I believe God will help me complete this book and will not falter on His promise.

Jesus refers to faith as the size of a mustard seed, one of the smallest seeds mentioned in the Bible. If we all possessed this level of faith, our lives and the world would differ vastly from what we currently experience. With this level of faith, nothing would be impossible. Faith, hope, and love are the three theological virtues of Christian belief, with faith regarded as the Primary Virtue. After reflecting on the message I received, I decided to keep writing and leave everything in God's hands. God entrusted me with completing this book, so I need to have faith that I can fulfil this assignment.

I wish to express my gratitude to Fr. Michael Payyapilly VC and Fr. Roni George VC for their spiritual guidance and support from the first day I entered the temporary Retreat Centre in Lutana Road to the present day at the new premises in Henson's Road.

I invite you to walk with me on this journey of Faith.

Chapter 3

A Life Shaped by Faith and Loss

I was born in Durban and grew up in Sydenham, South Africa. I am the youngest of eight children, with three brothers and four sisters. My mum passed away when I was two months old, and my dad, siblings, and grandmother raised me. Life was tough back then, as my dad had to raise eight kids independently.

I have two brothers and one sister who are still alive today. My dad remarried when I was ten, which brought us two stepsisters and three stepbrothers. My stepmother and one stepbrother are still living. My eldest sister was already married when my dad remarried, so she moved out of our family. home to build her own life with her husband. My second-eldest sister got married two years after my dad remarried. With two families living together, our house was always full, but we got along most of the time and faced difficulties like any other family.

We were raised as staunch Catholics and were fortunate to live next door to the Catholic Church and the Primary School I attended. The orphanage was also located on the same property. As a young child, I loved going to church and would often role-play the Mass with my sister and friends.

The church, school, and orphanage took up three blocks of land, and our house was right next to the school and the orphanage playgrounds. I would go through an opening in the hedge to get to school and church, as it was quicker than walking down to the gate to enter the school premises. I often left for school when the bell rang and still managed to arrive on time.

At about 14 years of age, I experienced the first loss of my dearest brother. I say first, as I was a baby when my mother died. This was the most devastating news for any parent and siblings to hear. I vividly remember the day and what I was doing when we received the news.

It was Holy Saturday, 28th March 1975, at around 4:00 p.m. We were cooking for the next day, Easter Sunday, and preparing to attend the Easter Vigil Mass. I was about to take a bath when the police knocked on our front door and informed us that my brother had been in a motor accident and had died.

He had been working away from home in Johannesburg and was travelling home to spend Easter with the family. On his previous trip back home, he had been planning his 21st birthday party, which would have taken place in August 1975, the same year he died.

By the time I finished bathing, the police had left, and I received the devastating news. I was young and could not comprehend that my brother would never return home. I loved my brother dearly, and his loss was immense for my family, especially my dad. I can only imagine what my dad went through during that time. No parent should have to bury their child.

That Easter was the saddest and most painful one I can remember. I do not travel during the Easter break or enjoy being on the roads then, as I always recall the memory of my brother's death. Easter is the most significant event in the history of the Catholic Church. Since I was a young girl, I have attended Mass during Holy Week, from Palm Sunday to Wednesday evening and Thursday to Sunday morning.

Thursday was the Mass of the Lord's Supper, where Jesus washed the apostles' feet and instituted the Eucharist. He humbled himself, as Peter says, "You shall never wash my feet". Jesus replies, "If I do not wash you, you have no part in me." Simon Peter said to him, "Lord, not my feet only but also my hands and head!" (John 13:8-9).

This is the night that Jesus is betrayed by Judas and denied three times by Peter. Jesus goes to the garden of Gethsemane and prays earnestly, and his sweat becomes like significant drops of blood. After the Mass, the ladies stay back for the first session as we pray in front of the Altar of Repose, while the men pray from 10:00 p.m. to midnight.

The next day was Good Friday, the Lord's Passion, a day when we contemplate the readings from the time Jesus prayed in the Garden of Gethsemane, where he was arrested and taken to trial. He is then sentenced to death on the cross for a crime he never committed. He was innocent, yet he took the punishment for us.

He had the power to stop this, but he chose not to, as He was obedient to the will of his Heavenly Father.

As a young girl, I understood the pain and suffering Jesus had to endure because of us, which filled me with deep remorse as I was still trying to let go of the Good Friday Service. Saturday marked the Easter Vigil Mass, where we began in darkness with readings from the Old Testament leading into the New Testament. Then, Easter Mass commenced. Sunday was the Mass of Resurrection.

A day to celebrate the Risen Lord. It is the time of year when you are taken back in time, and you begin to walk with Jesus from the moment He enters Jerusalem for the Passover until His resurrection. This is the moment to reflect on the pain and suffering of our Lord and how obedient he was to His Father in heaven, that He gave his life for us on the cross. The cross that bore our sins and our transgressions. It was a time of deep reflection, as I looked at my life, felt remorse for my sins, and asked God for His forgiveness and mercy.

Then Sunday arrives, and we enter into a state of joy because the Lord has risen and is truly alive. We know He loves us as He offered His life for us on the cross. Jesus tells us, "Greater love has no man than this, that a man lay down his life for his friends." (John 15:13). Little did I know that I would lose my brother that weekend. He died on Good Friday. May his soul rest in peace. I love and miss you, my brother.

I later became involved in the Girl Guide movement, starting as a Brownie, then progressing to Girl Guides, and eventually becoming a Ranger. The Motto of a Guild Guide is to Be Prepared, which guided me throughout my childhood and adulthood. During these years, we learnt many survival skills, such as how to tie knots. We also went camping and were taught how to survive in the outdoors.

We also learned how to work in a team and respect others, which helped us grow into mature young teenagers. We had wonderful times while learning. My dad was a Scout Master and later became the Chairperson of the Scouting Committee. All my brothers were part of the Scout Movement, which is how I became involved in the Girl Guide Movement.

As I grew up, I attended many retreats that I enjoyed. My spiritual life was at its peak as I deeply desired to learn more about Jesus. I began attending Mass on Wednesday nights, in addition to my Sunday obligation, and genuinely enjoyed the services. The church was filled every week. We had a second church that served the people in the Sydenham area. Previously a small church, it was later demolished and rebuilt into a new, larger church that serves as the main church in our Sydenham district. The main church is St Anne's, while the secondary church is St Theresa's.

There was a time when St Anne's held special prayers at 4:00 a.m. from Monday to Friday for one week. My friend and I would walk about 3 km to attend these prayers. It felt safe to walk at that hour back then. When I got home, my dad would be leaving for work, and we were still attending high school.

During this time, I decided I wanted to become a nun. I wrote a letter to my dad and stepmother explaining my desire. They discussed it with me and suggested I pursue a career first, then decide if I still wanted to become a nun. I also wrote to Fr Bux, the priest who conducted the retreats, sharing my wish to become a nun. He referred my letter to the nuns of the Augustinian Order, who oversaw the orphanage next door to our home.

They later reached out to me to ask about my interest in becoming a nun. I then had a chat with our parish priest, who inquired if I'd prefer to work with the missionaries. I declined, as the idea didn't appeal to me at the time. I wasn't keen on working in remote areas, and the thought of being apart from my family frightened me, so I gave up on the idea of becoming a nun.

After finishing school, I began attending parties and enjoying my youth. My dad was strict, so we had to be home by 10:00 p.m. whenever we went out, which felt too early as we grew older. The saying at that time was, "That was the time the party was only starting." I had a few friendships that were not serious. At that time, we were too afraid to have serious relationships as we feared what our parents would say. The appropriate age to bring a boy home was twenty-one, as we were handed a key at our twenty-first birthday parties, representing our transition to adulthood.

When I left school, I thought I would become a nurse, so I sent an application form to the hospital. While I was waiting, I decided to work in a hairdressing salon. My boss, the owner, offered me an apprenticeship, so I decided to accept her offer. I completed my apprenticeship and became a qualified hairdresser.

In 1986, I got married and later had two daughters. After a few years of marriage, we decided to consider immigrating to Australia, so I applied and left it in God's hands. If it were His will for us to immigrate to Australia, I knew that He would pave a clear path for us and remove any obstacles we might encounter. To my amazement, the entire immigration application process went so smoothly that I realised God's hand was upon us.

The process took an average of two years, and our application took just that long. Throughout this journey, I continued to trust in God. Our application was successful, and I believed it was God's will for us to immigrate to Australia. We had six months to leave the country. Once we learned that our application was successful, I began fervently praying to the Lord, asking Him to help us find a house close to the school, a bus stop, a church, and the shops. He heard my prayers and fulfilled every one of my requests. I had faith and trust in God; He would hear and answer my prayers. We left three months early to coincide with the Australian school holidays. It was my wish for my daughters to start school at the beginning of the Third School Term.

On July 7, 1997, we landed in Sydney at 7 p.m. I will never forget that day, as we were about to embark on a new journey in a foreign country. Every time I look at the date and time, I realise how Blessed we were, as the date reads.

(7-7-97 @ 7 PM). Seven is God's number. A new chapter in our lives begins.

Chapter 4

Prayers, Loss, and Grace in a New Home

We arrived in a country we had never previously visited. From the moment we walked out of the airport, we were stepping into a new era of life. We lived with my sister-in-law for three weeks while we settled in and arranged all our affairs.

We were blessed with two daughters who any parent would be proud of. When they were still small, they left their friends and family to start a new life here in Australia. They did not fully understand then and missed their life in South Africa for the first few years.

Before I left, I prayed to live near the school, church, bus stop, and shops. The Lord kindly blessed us with my request, as everything is within walking distance. We also have easy access to the main highways. My husband and I were both blessed with jobs.

My husband later left the company he was working for and decided to become self-employed. After renting for about eighteen months, the house was put up for sale. We were fortunate enough to have the deposit for the home, so we put in an offer, and we were successful. By the Grace of God, we could remain in the same house. I couldn't see myself going through the process of packing up and trying to find another rental home. The Lord answered my prayers by providing us with the correct location and fulfilling everything I had prayed for.

My kids attended our Parish Primary School, located on the same property as the church. They then progressed to the Catholic High School in our parish. We worked extremely hard to send our kids to school and to pay off our mortgage. By the grace of God, we achieved a great deal. They soon settled in, formed wonderful friendships, and remain friends to this very day. Both did exceedingly well; they are now married with kids and have their own homes.

I used to go out most weekends with friends from work or my husband. The lifestyle in Australia was quite different from what I was used to in South Africa. Once I got married and had children, I had no social life; we mostly attended family gatherings.

In the first eighteen months in Australia, I was thrilled when my parents reached out and said they were planning a trip to visit us. I knew it would reassure my dad to see me settled in a new country.

As the youngest, regardless of my age, I was still regarded as the baby in the family. It was wonderful to have my parents and sister at our new home. My dad and stepmum were pleased to see us happy and settled in our adopted country, which gave them peace of mind. They all enjoyed a fantastic holiday here in Australia.

In September 2001, I made my first visit back home. The week I was leaving, terrorists attacked the Twin Towers, and I was due to fly out on Saturday, which happened on Tuesday, the 11th of September 2001. I had never felt so anxious about flying until that day. I remember watching it on television when I returned home from work that day.

I could not comprehend what was happening. I was in shock and crying as everything unfolded before me. It was tough to take in, and it made me feel sick to the core watching the two Towers destroyed in a matter of minutes. So many lives were lost, and just as many were injured. A part of me wanted to cancel, but the excitement of seeing my family outweighed my anxiety about flying.

Another reason I chose not to cancel my flight was that my sister was extremely ill, and I wanted to see her and spend quality time with her before she deteriorated. I wanted to cherish good memories of her, knowing I might never see her again. Despite her illness, she planned a surprise birthday party for me right under my nose, and I had no clue what she was up to. She had the help of one of her friends and my best mate. It was a brilliant party, and seeing all my friends and family together was lovely. She passed away on 12 January 2005. I managed to have a safe trip to South Africa and returned home safely.

I promised myself that when I immigrated to Australia, I would allow myself five years to settle in and get accustomed to being away from my family and living in a new country. Within two years, I was extremely comfortable and loved our newly adopted country. The next few years were to be very painful for me.

After I lost my sister, I also lost my dad on 11 January 2007 and my second eldest sister on 6 June 2009. My eldest sister died on 18 February 2015. I was fortunate that my sister was able to visit me from South Africa when my eldest sister passed away. We were both shocked and devastated. I felt grateful that God arranged for my sister to be with me during this sad time.

We were fortunate to have each other to mourn and comfort one another at the loss of our eldest sister. During this time, I was actively involved in Couples for Christ. They would come to our home every night, praying the Rosary and Novena for the Dead with my family. They provided us with great support. I am unsure how I would have coped without their prayers and support. The loss of my family had a devastating effect on me. I had no other family here as I was the only one who immigrated to Australia. My sister immigrated to Scotland about eighteen months after I left South Africa. Through my loss, I knew I could turn to God for help in overcoming the pain I felt. In the later years of my life, there were many times I felt depressed and saddened by the loss of my dad and siblings, but it was only through prayer and our Lord Jesus Christ that I managed to overcome the pain caused by my loss. Jesus says, "Come to me, all who labor and are heavy laden, and I will give you rest. (Matthew 11:28).

A tribute to my dad

Before I immigrated to Australia in the nineties, Visionary Vicka Ivankovic Mijatovic and Fr. Slavko Barbaric OFM from Medjugorje visited our main church, St Anne's Parish in Sydenham, Durban. After Mass, while saying the rosary led by Vicka, Our Lady appeared to her, and then she conveyed the message to us through Fr. Slavko. The Mass, talk, and rosary were recorded on a VCR cassette, which I brought to Australia. One day, I decided to lend the video cassette to our assistant parish priest, Fr. Peter Tangey OSA. He kept it with him for a few years. Little did I know that God had a plan in place for the years to come.

In 2007, Fr. Peter was assigned to the Augustinian Formation House in Brookvale. While packing his belongings, he came across my video cassette. My dad passed away on the 11th of January 2007, and on the day of the funeral, I was feeling upset and restless and was praying, trying to be there spiritually. I reflected on all the beautiful times we had with my dad from childhood to adulthood. I was happy to have had the opportunity to go back home and spend time with him before he deteriorated. On that day, there was a knock at my front door, and to my surprise, when I opened it, Fr. Peter stood before me. I had no idea that he was coming to visit that day. My dad's name is also Peter.

He had come to return the video cassette as he was leaving our parish. He was the last person I expected to see. When God saw my pain, He acted instantly and sent Fr. Peter to visit me. The Spirit of the Lord chose that particular day, which was no coincidence, and whispered to Fr. Peter to go to my place, to be with me and pray with me. God is so great; He knows exactly what we are going through. He is always there for us, waiting for us to turn to Him. We started talking, and I told him that God had sent him to me, as it was the day my dad was being buried. The Lord knew my heart and how I felt, as I couldn't travel at the time due to illness.

Only He knows the inner depths of our hearts, the part that no one else knows. Be mindful that He knows everything about us, having created us. "For you formed my inward parts, you knitted me together in my mother's womb." (Psalm 139:13).

Fr. Peter encouraged me to talk about my dad, and I recalled all the lovely memories I have of him. He was highly respected in the community as a kind and devoted father. Although he was strict, he was also very loving and warm-hearted. He had to raise eight children on his own until he remarried when I was ten. My eldest sister was thirteen when my mother passed away. Fr. Peter prayed with me, and I felt much better and more at peace when he left. I will always remember this day.

I felt so touched and blessed that the Lord arranged for Fr. Peter to come to me when I was mourning the loss of my dad. God always hears and answers our prayers and sends human angels to help us when we need them most. Prayer is powerful; Jesus tells us, "Therefore, I tell you, whatever you ask in prayer, believe that you receive it, and you will.". (Mark 11: 24)

RIP

Chapter 5

The Healing Power of Faith

"THOU HAS FORMED US FOR THYSELF, AND OUR HEARTS ARE RESTLESS TILL THEY FIND RESTS IN THEE."

From 2008 to 2010, I decided to study through Oten, doing a Business Administration Course, which I enjoyed as I love learning new things and enjoying challenges. 2010 was a challenging yet fruitful year, as my husband and I were blessed with our first grandson. He has brought such joy into our lives, and children are a blessing from God.

As Jesus tells us:

"But when Jesus saw it was indignant, and said to them," Let the children come to me, do not hinder them; for to such belongs the kingdom of God. Truly, I say to you, whoever does not receive the kingdom of God like a child shall not enter it.' And he took them in his arms and blessed them, laying his hands upon them." (Mark 10:14-16).

As the years went by, I faced numerous challenges in my life. At times, it felt as though I was wandering in darkness. My life was spiralling out of control, and I was suffering from the effects of stress. There was a period when I had a delayed reaction to the deaths of my dad and sisters. I was heading towards depression, but I quickly had to pull myself out of it because I didn't want it to take over my life. I would pray and ask God for help, as I wasn't pleased with how I felt. There was a time when I didn't attend Mass every Sunday, and I felt terrible about that. I was utterly lost in the world.

In my most challenging times, I turned to God for help. One day at home, I was feeling anxious and stressed, so I went down on my knees with my hands stretched out, crying out to God to heal me and to help me. I trusted in God to heal me. That day, I surrendered everything to God and allowed Him to take control of my life. I felt so much better after praying and surrendering everything to God.

I decided to make an appointment to see my doctor. I was suffering the effects of stress. He suggested I get involved in my parish and join a prayer group, which will help me. I put my name down for a family prayer group, but nobody contacted me.

Many months later, a family friend asked my husband and me if we would like to join a family prayer group called Couples for Christ, which I had signed up for a few months earlier. This is a Charismatic group in our parish. He explained everything that happens in the group. We would have to attend the Christian Life Programme over four Sunday afternoons. God's timing is perfect; He plans everything flawlessly and sends human angels to help us fulfil His plans. Joining Couples for Christ was the best decision for my husband and me at the time. We held weekly Household Prayer Meetings, with each couple taking turns hosting the meetings at home.

My life was beginning to change; I could feel the spirit of God moving within me, and healing was beginning. I started to rediscover God and our Lord Jesus Christ. Our prayer meetings focused on the Sunday Gospel for that weekend. Once a year, each state has the opportunity to host a conference. Our first conference was held in Sydney, and then we attended our second one in Queensland on the Gold Coast. Both were spiritual and uplifting; you could feel God's presence filling the hall, and we also had a great deal of fun. Each district had to perform an act; the best act won first prize.

It was beautiful to witness so many people praising and worshipping God. We had Mass each day, and the Bishop celebrated the closing Mass on the last day of the conference.

God found the perfect group for us to join. Everybody welcomed us with open arms and made us feel like part of the group. Through Couples for Christ, I began to heal, and my life started to fall back into place. I have joined a few ministries in our parish and remain actively involved. I could see the hand of God working in my life, and healing was beginning to take place.

We face challenges in our lives that we must confront head-on, and if you are not strong in your faith, you will find it exceedingly difficult to overcome these hurdles; it is only through the grace of God and through faith that you can succeed.

We might feel completely alone during these times, but we often forget that God is always with us. He is with us in good times and in despair when we believe there is no one to turn to; God is always there, ready for us to reach out to Him. He is the most loving, forgiving, merciful, kind-hearted, and the only one we can truly trust.

"Thou has formed us for Thyself, and our hearts are restless until they find rest in Thee" (St Augustine of Hippo Confessions 1,1.5). I find this to be so true. Without inner peace, faith, and trust in God, we will always feel restless unless we ask God for the peace only, He can provide. "I have said this to you, that in me you might have peace. In the world you have tribulation; but be of good cheer; I have overcome the world." (John 16:33).

Amid my tribulations, God helped me through His Word, the Holy Bible. I started reading the Bible more often, and God revealed everything that was happening in my life at that time through His Word. I began to realise that God sees everything; He knows our pain, sorrow, and the hurt we face. I was startled initially, but then I became ecstatic when I realised God was with me and understood what I had experienced. He was giving me that inner peace that only He could provide. Once I recognised that God was working in my life and opening my eyes to all that was occurring, I was on the road to recovery.

I made an appointment with one of our priests, spoke to him, and asked him to hear my confession. I felt healed, unburdened, and ready to start a new chapter in my life. Sometimes, we must face trials and hit rock bottom before rediscovering our connection with God. I have always known and loved God, but I have fallen many times along my journey. Only by God's grace did I rise and continue on the path He has planned for me.

Now and then, I was weakening every time I recalled the past, as I could not let go, and I could not forgive the ones who hurt me. It is like a wound that festers internally when forgiveness is not extended. It feels like you're walking around with a block of cement attached to your shoulders, and all it's doing is weighing you down. To be free, you must free yourself from the heavy burdens you carry, and only then can you feel much lighter and free to move forward, allowing God to take control of your life. Only then will you start to see the change within you.

No matter how often you fall, pray and ask God to give you the strength to carry your cross. "Rejoice always, pray constantly, give thanks in all circumstances; for this is the will of God in Christ Jesus for you." (1 Thessalonians 5: 16-18).

Chapter 6

Faith in the Face of Fear

This is how the book A Woman of Faith came to be written. My belief, faith, and trust in God the Father and our Lord Jesus Christ have led me to write this book.

After emerging from the darkness, I began to recover. In April 2014, our parish held a Healing Mass led by Rev Fr. Michael Payyapilly VC. When I saw it advertised in our parish news bulletin, I knew I had to attend, as I had never been to one before, so my husband and I both went. It was all unfamiliar to me. We started with praise and worship, followed by a talk based on Scripture readings. After the talk, we celebrated Mass. Following the Mass, we participated in Healing Adoration. It was during this Mass that change came over me, as I had never felt so touched by the Power of the Holy Spirit.

While Fr. Michael was talking, I saw a quick flash of an image on the Sanctuary just behind the Lectern of a white garment, which looked pure white and seemed like a breeze was blowing it and forming folds at the bottom. I remember saying to myself that it looked whiter than snow. Not long after, I heard Fr. Michael repeat those exact words during Adoration, as though the Lord was validating through Fr. Michael what I had seen and the words that came to me when I saw the garment.

It was my first experience of a Healing Mass, and I thoroughly enjoyed it. The seed had been planted. I had no idea that God chose me to be at this Healing Mass, as it was from this Mass that the Lord guided me on the path, He wanted me to walk towards this journey of Faith. We never know when He will tap us on the shoulder and ask us to go out and be His witness. I have always been grateful to Fr. Michael for accepting our parish's invitation to visit.

I soon realised that Fr. Michael was a religious priest from the Vincentian Order and the Director of a retreat Centre in Somersby, NSW. When my husband and I returned home, I told him I wanted to attend a Retreat.

I had no idea where Somersby was until I realised it was on the Central Coast, which took about an hour and a half to drive in good traffic back then. The roads have since improved with the construction of a new tunnel, saving 15 minutes of travel time. I thought my husband would say no, as it was too far to travel. To my surprise, he said we could go. When God wants to send you somewhere, He will plan everything to make it possible for you to get where you need to be. To my delight, my husband, niece, and I attended the retreat. The live-in retreats started on Friday at 9 a.m. and finished on Sunday at 4 p.m.

Our first Retreat was a Marian Retreat in May 2014. Being new to Praise and Worship, Preaching the Word of God, and Healing Eucharistic Adoration, I had no idea what to expect.

On the second day of the retreat, I was captivated by the picture of Jesus behind the altar. To my astonishment, I realised that the white garment Jesus wore in the poster was identical to the image I had seen on the altar at the Healing Mass in our parish, conducted by Fr. Michael Payyapilly VC, which appeared as if a gentle breeze had rustled through the garment. (see the front pages of the book)

The only difference was that I did not see a red sash, as shown in the picture behind the altar. A few weeks before I went on retreat, I kept getting flashes of a white garment and being stopped by a police officer. I was pulled over a few weeks prior to attending the retreat because I was driving slightly over the speed limit. It was the first time a police officer had stopped me since we arrived in the country. On the second day, I realised Fr. Michael was the priest wearing a white cassock. During that first retreat, all three came to a realisation.

On Saturday night, we had Healing Adoration, and I was amazed because I had never experienced anything like it. We were taken back in time to our mother's womb, to the moment we were born. We revisited the various stages of our lives, recalling the hurt and pain we had endured and asking God to heal the inner wounds that had hurt us and prevented us from experiencing His grace.

This was exceedingly difficult for me at the time, as my mother passed away two months after I was born. This was the first time I had experienced something like this. As Fr. Michael was going through the various stages, I was sobbing as this wound, which I suppressed for so many years, was suddenly opened, and I had to confront it.

In my lifetime, I never got to say the words mummy or mum. For some reason, this always saddened me. It took me several retreats for this wound to heal. I always think of my mum and got to know her through my dad and siblings. She was a good mother, brilliant, good with her hands, and well-respected in the community. I take after her in a few ways. We learned how to let go and forgive those who caused us pain.

I will honestly say that that night, I cried bitterly, and it escalated to the 'ugly' cry. I was sitting at the front and was probably heard from the back of the Chapel. Earlier, I mentioned how I was carrying a lot of hurt and unforgiveness; even though I thought I had let go, I realised I had not fully released my burdens that night. Those inner wounds were reopened, and I became aware that I still clung to my pain, and that for me to heal, I had to forgive completely and let go.

We all had the opportunity to attend the Sacrament of Reconciliation on Saturday. I went to confession and received counselling, which helped me understand what I needed to do to achieve complete forgiveness and healing. When I got home, I felt spiritually renewed and liberated from the heavy burden I had carried for many years.

"For if you forgive men their trespasses, your heavenly Father also will forgive you; but if you do not forgive men their trespasses, neither will your Father forgive your trespasses." (Matthew 6:14-15).

After attending that retreat, which I loved, I continued to participate in retreats twice a month, which included weekend retreats and those on the last Sunday, the remainder of that year and the next. Today, I am actively volunteering. I could sense Jesus working in my life, and change was beginning to take hold of me.

Listening to Fr. Michael Payyapilly preach the Word of God during the retreats increased my desire to learn more about Jesus. Before attending retreats, I hardly read the Old Testament, but I learned so much from the talks that I developed a passionate love for the Word of God. Each time I attended retreats, I fell in love with God and our Saviour Jesus Christ.

I leaned on Jesus more as my passion grew more robust. This Bible verse is written on the bottom of the picture of Jesus in the Divine Retreat Centre, "Come to me, all you who labor and are heavy laden, and I will give you rest." (Matthew 11:28).

When we let go and hand everything over to Jesus, He takes charge and starts to heal our inner wounds. We need to trust in Him first. We often cling to our baggage because we believe we can manage it on our own. Jesus patiently waits for us to come to Him, as He tells us: "Ask, and it will be given you; seek, and you will find; knock, and it will be opened to you. For everyone who asks receives, and he who seeks finds, and to him who knocks it will be opened." (Matthew 7:7-8).

A Glimpse of the Divine at 3 A.M

WRITE IN A BOOK EVERYTHING THAT HAS HAPPENED TO YOU.

For some time, I had been waking up between 3:00 a.m. and 3:30 a.m. and reciting the Divine Mercy Chaplet during this time, as it is considered the hour for prayer. While praying on the 13th of October 2014, at approximately 3 a.m., I distinctly heard the voice of the Lord say, "Catholic Church." I was trembling, and my heart was racing, so I offered the Divine Mercy Chaplet for the Catholic Church.

I sleep with the Rosary under my pillow so I can find it easily when I wake at 3 a.m. Another reason I keep my Rosary close is that it provides me comfort and assurance that the Blessed Mother is watching over me. As a young girl, I always slept with the Rosary under my pillow, and I find it exceedingly challenging to fall asleep without it. I lost my mum when I was a baby, so as a young child, I always turned to Our Blessed Mother when I felt afraid.

When I arose in the morning, I prayed and asked the Lord, if it were Him could He reveal it to me through the Holy Bible, as Jesus speaks to us through the Word of God. I went to my prayer table, and the first page my eyes fell upon was (v 7) "It is good to guard the secret of a king, but gloriously to reveal the works of God and with fitting honour to acknowledge him." (v 20) "And now, Bless the Lord upon the earth and give thanks to God, for I am ascending to him who sent me. Write in a book everything that has happened to you." (Tobit 12: 1-22).

I read the whole chapter. Jesus, through His Word, was telling me to reveal and acknowledge that what I heard was God's voice, to give Him honour and respect, and to make it known to others. On October 14th, 2014, I posted this on my Facebook page, asking people to pray for the Catholic Church.

I don't post much on my Facebook page, maybe once or twice a year, but because this was such a clear message, I felt compelled to share it. I take this verse as further confirmation of the book I am writing, as I am constantly praying to Our Lord for His inspiration and validation as its author.

I always pray for the Catholic Church, as it is under attack by the evil one. The Lord has asked us to pray for the Catholic Church, so I encourage you to make this a daily prayer, as the Church truly needs our prayers. The Divine Mercy Chaplet Prayer is recited at 3 p.m. daily, the hour we commemorate the Passion of Jesus.

I pray that you take this message seriously as I speak the truth and make it your daily prayer to pray fervently for the Holy Catholic Church to be protected from the destruction of the evil one. I also ask that you pray for all priests, the Pope, and all members of the religious community.

Most mornings, I am awake between 3 a.m. and 4 a.m. I find this a beautiful time to pray and spend time with God. Sometimes, I recite the Rosary and the Divine Mercy Chaplet if I cannot sleep. Do not pray only for yourself during this hour, as it is usually offered for others who need prayers. When you start praying, God will inspire you to pray for those who need your prayers during that hour.

On another occasion, on January 2nd, 2015, at 4:15 a.m., I was awakened and heard the voice of the Lord say, "Pray to the Lord. It is the Lord who speaks."

When I heard this, my heart was racing, so I got out of bed. My legs were weak as I was shaking and in shock. I went to my prayer table to pray and opened my bible. As it opened, my eyes fell upon, "So then let us not sleep, as others do, but let us keep awake and be sober." It tells us of the coming of the Lord, to be awake and not sleep as others do. "Rejoice always, pray constantly, give thanks in all circumstances; for this is the will of God in Christ Jesus for you. Do not quench the Spirit, do not despise prophesying, but test everything; hold fast what is good, abstain from every form of evil." (1 Thessalonians 5:1-28).

I must clarify that I've never heard voices in my head on any other occasions. This is spiritual, and Jesus confirms that He is speaking. It differs from the times when the Spirit of the Lord speaks, as that comes from the heart, and you don't hear an audible voice. These are the two occasions I heard the voice of Jesus. His voice was soft and gentle. I wasn't scared, but more in shock as I tried to understand what I had heard. My body felt like it was on fire, and my heart was racing, so I immediately got out of bed and went to pray and read my Bible.

Prayer is powerful. It is a dialogue, not a monologue. It's just between you and God. Open your heart to Him, for He knows all your troubles. He wants you to speak to Him. God knows what you want before you ask Him, but He waits for you to come to Him. While praying and talking to God is important, sitting in silence and listening to God speak to you in the depths of your heart is equally vital. God wants you to pray constantly and give thanks in all circumstances. Don't just pray when things aren't going well for you. Remember God in your joyful moments as well.

A Dream That Spoke of God's Grace

In the early hours of 17th March 2019, I had a dream related to reading the Gospel. At the Lectern, two Altar Servers stood on either side, each holding a large candle. Just before the priest was about to read the gospel, I awoke saying these words: "Those who listen will be gracious unto God." I had never read or heard these words being said before this. I felt inspired to write them down. When I looked at the clock, it was 4:30 a.m.

I never entirely understood these words until recently, when I found this verse: "Therefore the Lord waits to be gracious to you; therefore, he exalts himself to show mercy to you. For the Lord is a God of Justice; blessed are all those who wait for him." (Isaiah 30:18).

The Bible is the true Word of God, and He speaks to us through His Word. God is telling me that He wants to pour out His grace upon me, and He is a merciful and just God to those who seek His mercy, believe in Him, and have hope in Him. He will also pardon us from all our faults and lead us on the path of righteousness while we wait for Him.

He shows mercy to all who seek His forgiveness and justice to all who wait for Him. We need to listen to the voice of God deep within our hearts. Don't let the voice of the evil one deceive you. Open your Bible and ask God to speak to you through His Word when you're in doubt. He will answer you, but you must believe that He communicates through His Word, the Holy Bible.

"Let your speech always be gracious, seasoned with salt, so that you may know how you ought to answer everyone." (Colossians 4: 6).

We should always be mindful of how we speak to others. Just as salt flavours food, our speech should be flavoured with the aroma of Christ when we talk to others.

Chapter 7

The Diagnosis That Shook Us Both

In our second year of attending retreats, my husband was diagnosed with prostate cancer. The news was devastating for us. We were both dealing with our own personal struggles because of this diagnosis. We were both in shock, and I was unsure how to manage the situation.

Only God knew the road we would have to walk. He lovingly mapped out our journey so well, as only He knew His plans for us. He understood we would need all the strength to face the journey ahead. He instilled in our hearts the desire to attend the retreats every month, and through attending them, we grew stronger in our faith, which in turn helped us develop complete trust in God.

During the retreats, we had guest speakers who preached the Word of God and shared their testimonies about what God had done for them, including how God had healed and transformed their lives. Around this time, Brother Thomas would sometimes preach, and one day, he said, "There is someone here who has cancer." After his talk, my husband approached him and mentioned that he had cancer and would need an operation. Brother Thomas told him, "Don't worry, you will be healed within three months."

We were both astonished by what had happened that day. We both felt relieved knowing that the Lord would heal my husband. I don't think we would have coped the way we did had it not been for our total trust and faith in God.

After several visits with doctors and specialists, it was decided that they would remove the prostate. Thank God the operation went well, and he was home within two days. Although the operation went well, the psychological damage was done. Lots of prayers were offered for us, especially during this time. After the operation, some side effects occurred, but fortunately, they did not last long. We had heard a few stories of others who were not as fortunate as we were in terms of a smooth recovery.

We could not wait to get back to the Retreat Centre as we had not attended any retreats when my husband had his operation. We realised that it was three months after the operation, and my husband was fully recovered. I told him that I would inform Fr. Michael about his recovery, as revealed to us by Br. Thomas.

When Fr. Michael received the email, he asked if we would like to give a testimony. During the last Sunday retreat that month, my husband shared his testimony accompanied by me, in front of about 250-300 people. Although we felt nervous, having never spoken in front of so many before, God took away our fear and anxiety, and my husband gave a beautiful testimony. We chose to do this to acknowledge God's healing power. God was great; He kept His word and fulfilled His promise. It was fitting that we publicly shared His love and the healing He bestowed upon my husband.

Jesus heals ten lepers and only one goes back to thank him (...) v15 onwards; Then one of them, when he saw that he was healed, turned back, praising God with a loud voice, and he fell on his face at Jesus' feet giving him thanks (...) v17 Then said Jesus," Were not ten cleansed? Where are the nine? Was no one found to return and give praise to God except this foreigner?" And he said to him. "Rise and go your way: your faith has made you well." (Luke 17:11-19).

We faithfully attend retreats each month. I find them spiritually healing for my mind, body, and soul. God is a true Healer. Retreats also help me foster a closer relationship with God and experience His omniscient presence around me. My prayer life has deepened, and I've begun drawing closer to God. I put God above everything else; He is the Head of our home. I immensely love God the Father and His Son, our Lord Jesus Christ.

A Vision I Never Expected

In 2015, we attended a weekend retreat, and during Eucharistic Healing Adoration, Fr. Michael said, "Some of us would have visions in silhouette." I never gave it a second thought, as I never visualised in my life that I would have a vision. I remember this day very clearly; during the Healing Service, I had a vision of the Hand of God reaching out to me. His hand was remarkably close to me, within reaching distance. To try and describe it, the space was very brightly lit, and directly in the centre was an arm in silhouette reaching down from above towards me. The hand was in an open gesture, and I was trying to reach out and touch God's hand.

I felt so at peace and happy that God was reaching out to me; I was in awe and wonder, and I couldn't stop smiling during the vision. It felt like I was the only person in the Chapel reaching out to grasp His hand at that moment. It must have lasted about one to one and a half minutes. This was the first vision I had ever experienced, and what a beautiful experience it was. I was blown away, as I never thought I would have a vision in my lifetime, especially after what I had seen.

In January 2024, the Spirit of God reminded me of this vision, which I had forgotten to include in my notes for this book. This is an accurate account of what I saw and is not exaggerated in form or content. Believe

Chapter 8

Touching the Heart of the Holy Land

In 2016, my husband and I went on our first pilgrimage to the Holy Land, organised by our parish and accompanied by our parish priest, Fr. Michael Belonio OSA, as our Spiritual Director.

Since the plan was to leave from the Philippines, a friend asked my husband, me, and another couple we were travelling with if we would like to spend a week in the Philippines before our departure to the Holy Land. The plan was for all the pilgrims to meet in the Philippines and then fly to Egypt to start our pilgrimage. As they were originally from the Philippines, we decided to accept their offer, because they would be the best people to show us around their country. So, we all stayed at their family home. We were delighted with this offer as we had never visited the Philippines before.

They took us to the Basilica Minore del Santo Niño de Cebu. The statue is one of the oldest surviving Catholic relics in the Philippines and is believed to have miraculous powers. I am fortunate to have one in my home. We visited the Simala Shrine in Cebu, where the statue of Our Lady is known to weep. We also visited the Seminary in Cebu, where Fr. Jesper OSA was assigned after leaving our parish a few months after his Ordination.

He was assigned to our parish as a brother, later ordained as a Deacon, and then ordained to the Priesthood. It was nice to visit him and see that the seminarians will one day be ordained as priests, as we desperately need more vocations to the Priesthood.

We then left for Egypt to begin our Pilgrimage and later we travelled to Jordan and Israel. We saw the Pyramids up close, which made us feel incredibly small. It's hard to fathom how they built such massive structures without our modern machinery. We also visited the place where Joseph and Mary hid with the infant Jesus until it was safe to return to Nazareth in the Holy Land. In Jordan, we visited Petra. It is so beautiful and rich in history. I couldn't walk down the gorge because of my knee injury, as it was a long walk. My friend and I paid for a horse and carriage to take us down. It was a fantastic experience.

The gorge is relatively narrow. You can still see how far the water reached when it flooded around 45 centuries ago. I was amazed at the colours inside the rocks as they revealed what they looked like when split in two.

We then journeyed on to Israel. I have always dreamed of visiting the Holy Land and walking in the footsteps of Jesus. Every place we visited, filled me with awe and wonder, as I realised this is where Jesus walked, preached, performed miracles, healed the sick, and ultimately died on the cross. As we drove towards our hotel in Israel, I saw a street sign with an arrow pointing to Jerusalem, since we were to visit Jerusalem the next day. Seeing that sign, tears filled my eyes as I remembered how Jesus wept over Jerusalem and the fate that awaited it.

The next day, we explored the Old City of Jerusalem within its walls. I felt incredibly sad as I looked at the pit where they held Jesus the night he was arrested. It was heartbreaking to see, and I couldn't help but cry. Walking along the Via Dolorosa was another moment that brought tears to my eyes as I carried the cross and followed the path Jesus had taken. The Church of the Holy Sepulchre was another site that moved me deeply; I felt so sad knowing I was standing on the very spot where Our Lord was crucified and laid to rest. I stood before the slab of stone where they laid Jesus after he died; it was a sorrowful and heartbreaking moment for me as I remembered the Passion of Christ.

I could only imagine the pain and agony he had to endure because of us. He paid the ultimate price. I thought of Mother Mary and how heartbreaking it would have been for her as she held his lifeless body in her arms. The words of Simeon rang true: "An arrow shall pierce your heart." My entire experience in the Holy Land was awe-inspiring and beautiful, and I hoped I could return one day.

Likewise, the Vatican was also one of the places I longed to visit. On November 22, 2016, we attended Mass there, marking the end of the Year of Mercy. Pope Francis closed the Door of Mercy, which was sealed until the next Jubilee Year. It was a truly remarkable moment to witness and be part of this significant event.

I never thought I'd visit the Vatican. Every time I saw the crowds on television, I thought I wouldn't be able to handle them, as I've never felt comfortable in large crowds. However, the crowds aren't as intimidating when you're there. The Vatican is divided into different sections, which makes it easier to see everything happening in the Sanctuary. We were lucky to be in the Basilica, so we had a good spot even though we stood throughout the entire Mass.

There are paths for the priest to walk and distribute Communion to the pilgrims, as well as areas where the Pope drives around in his Popemobile to greet them. I'm so glad I decided to visit the Vatican. It was such a brilliant experience. The Sistine Chapel was exquisite, with Michelangelo's paintings vividly coming to life, depicting the creation story, man's fall from God's grace, and the stories of Jesus.

We visited the Statue of David in Florence, one of Michelangelo's most renowned sculptures. I was amazed by the size and detail of the body, which was crafted with exquisite care. We learn about David in 1 Samuel 16 onwards. (The Lord appoints Samuel to go to Jesse the Bethlehemite to appoint his son David as King)

On our return from the Holy Land, we returned to the Philippines with the same couple, but this time, we spent about four days in Manila. Fr. Michael Belonio, originally from the Philippines, was also with us. We stayed one night on the premises where the Seminarians reside.

I remember the beds being so hard that I felt sorry for the seminarians who had to sleep on them. I heard the bell ring around 5 a.m. We went to Mass early in the morning, and it was lovely to see the seminarians actively participating. The choir sang beautifully. I felt happy that, once again, these seminarians would be ordained as priests one day, given the worldwide shortage of priests.

A Vision Beyond the Cross in Jerusalem

GREATER LOVE HAS NO MAN THAN THIS, THAT A
MAN LAY DOWN HIS LIFE FOR HIS FRIENDS.

In November 2017, one year after I visited the Holy Land, I was Blessed to revisit it. This time, my husband did not accompany me. The Divine Retreat Centre, Somersby, organised this pilgrimage for the volunteers.

I felt so blessed and privileged to have been given this opportunity again. I was privileged to see unfamiliar places I hadn't encountered on my previous trip. One of these was Jacobs Well, one of my favourite readings in John's gospel, chapter 4 – "Jesus and the Woman of Samaria." We visited the site where John the Baptist was beheaded and then went on to Mt Gerizim, where Joshua laid the twelve stones as he crossed over the Jordan. I was able to see things in a very different light this time around. Everything made more sense to me, as I could take my time and savour each moment on my pilgrimage.

On Tuesday, 21st November 2017, we visited the Old City of Jerusalem and walked along the Via Dolorosa. Once more, I felt profoundly moved and brought to tears as we walked and prayed the Stations of the Cross, stopping at each station to pray with the cross. I used the same cross I had bought in the Holy Land the previous year on pilgrimage.

It's very noisy, and there are many distractions while walking and praying the Stations of the Cross, but you must block out the noise and focus on what you are doing, remembering what Jesus was going through during this time. We walked in the shade, as it is enclosed, with shops lining either side of the walkway. Jesus walked in the hot sun. As I walked, sadness overcame me as I contemplated the stations and visualised what Jesus had to endure because of our transgressions. He was lashed until his skin ripped open and bled. He was pierced with a crown of thorns; he was tired and weak, which caused him to fall three times. He was rejected and despised, innocent unto death. His mother watched her Son in agony, and the pain in her heart would have been gut-wrenching, as there was nothing, she could do to help him. Scripture had to be fulfilled. He was obedient to the will of the Father unto death.

It was late afternoon, and we were returning to the hotel. While we were reciting the rosary on the bus, an open vision appeared before me. In the vision, I saw mountains that were the colour of sandstone, small to medium in size. Towards the bottom of the mountain, on the flat surface of the rock, I saw a face that I believe to be that of Jesus, blended into the rock. I hadn't seen these specific mountains while travelling through the Holy Land.

On the right-hand side, there was a huge wooden cross reaching towards the sky. I looked at the face briefly, but I felt as though I was not meant to gaze at the beauty of Our Lord for too long, but to focus my attention on the cross. The cross was the primary focus.

While looking at the vision, I realised that Jesus had seen us that day while praying the Stations of the Cross. He was saying that he was no longer on the cross and that the cross was His ultimate sacrifice for us. He bore our sins and paid the price. He is now with his Heavenly Father. It was through His obedience to Our Heavenly Father that Jesus gave his life for us.

(Vision on the bus in the Holy Land; see the front cover of the book)

We should never forget the significance of the cross. "He himself bore our sins in his body on the tree, that we might die to sin and live to righteousness. By his wounds, you have been healed." (1 Peter 2:24).

It is for our sins that Jesus had to be nailed to the cross with blood flowing from the top of his head, his hands, and his feet, and in his anguish, He cries out to The Father, "Father, forgive them for they know not what they do." To confirm that he had expired, they pierced his side with a spear, and blood and water flowed out from his side as an ocean of mercy for all humanity. "But he was wounded for our transgressions, he was bruised for our iniquities; upon him was the chastisement that made us whole, and with his stripes we are healed." (Isaiah 53:5).

"Greater love has no man than this, that a man lay down his life for his friends." (John 15:13).

I had a profound sense that Jesus was watching us that day. This was also the first thought that crossed my mind, and a feeling of peace washed over me. I didn't tell anyone that I had seen the vision during my pilgrimage. I spent time praying and reflecting on what I saw until the 8th of December 2017, when I emailed Fr. Rony Mukkuzhy VC about my experience.

We had our final Mass in Jerusalem the day before we departed from Israel. Before the Mass ended, we were all allowed to pray, giving thanks for our pilgrimage. When it was my turn to pray, as

I said, "I feel so blessed to be there on Pilgrimage for the second time and to be blessed with two priests guiding us," which were Fr. Roni Mukkuzhy VC, spiritual Director and Fr. Ronald Santosh O.F.M Cap, who was our tour guide.

I started crying as I felt filled with the Holy Spirit right at that moment. I felt so grateful and Blessed to be there. Our God is loving and compassionate, ready to pour His grace upon us.

After further reflection on the vision, I realise there are three main elements: the face of Jesus, the cross, and the mountains. Jesus revealed himself to me on a mountain. He often went to lonely places and frequently climbed mountains to pray, seeking to be one with his Heavenly Father.

He prayed and fasted for forty days on the Mount of Temptation. He was transfigured on Mount Tabor; He preached a powerful sermon, delivering the Beatitudes on the Mount of Beatitudes, and prayed in the Garden of Gethsemane on the Mount of Olives the night he was arrested. The cross is where he shed his blood for us and made the ultimate sacrifice, where he paid the price for our sins and transgressions.

Chapter 9

Prayers, Patience, and Unexpected Blessings

>   Knowledge is power. Knowledge shared is power multiplied.

My life was starting to get back on track, and in 2017, I decided to resume my studies. This time, I attended classes at TAFE to pursue a Certificate III and IV in Community Services. I was passionate about domestic violence, as every other day on the news, there was a case of domestic violence being reported.

I wanted to make a difference in the lives of victims, which broadened my career options. I never imagined I would find myself back in a classroom. Considering the pressure of assessment deadlines, I didn't think I had the motivation to study again. However, I passed and enjoyed my time at TAFE.

Towards the end of the course, we had a career day, and because my heart was set on working in the Domestic Violence field, I remember telling the teachers about the areas I didn't want to pursue, as I didn't feel I was suited for that work. Little did I know that one of the fields I said I wouldn't work in was where God found me employment. I learned that we often think we know what is best, but God knows what is best for us. He answers our prayers in His time and in the way He knows is best. With the zeal to study, I registered to enrol in a Diploma in Community Services. As I aspired to become a Case Manager specialising in Domestic Violence, my prospects depended on the outcome of my application for a subsidy. After I completed my course, our circumstances changed, and my husband asked if I could put my studies on hold and look for a job to help financially. I was conflicted about what to do until I attended a Retreat.

"Knowledge is power. Knowledge shared is power multiplied." (Robert Boyce. (n.d.). AZQuotes.com).

In 2018, there was a Volunteer Retreat, and that weekend, I prayed to God, asking Him whether I should continue my studies or start looking for a job. I wanted to study, but my husband wanted me to find a job. I felt confused and wasn't sure what to do.

At the Last Sunday Retreat in February, during Eucharistic Adoration, Father Rony VC said, "There are four people here whom God is Blessing with a job." I claimed that, praised, and thanked God. The following month, in March, at the Last Sunday Retreat, during Eucharistic Adoration, Father Rony again said that there are three people the Lord is Blessing with a job, and it is permanent. I then claimed it and thanking and praising God.

I hadn't started looking for work at that time. I soon realised that if the Lord were to bless me with a job, I needed to start applying for positions. I applied for two jobs in April 2018, but for the first one, I missed the deadline by a few minutes. Eventually, I heard back from them and was told that there were numerous applications, and they would get back to me.

I never heard from them again. For the second job I applied for, I received a call and had a phone interview. About a week later, I had a face-to-face interview, which progressed to the next stage, and the final step was the medical examination. I was so anxious that I hardly slept the night before the medical assessment.

It was a while before I heard from them, but in the meantime, I kept praying while waiting to hear the outcome. I didn't lose hope but surrendered everything to Jesus, as He told us. "Come to me, all who labor and are heavy laden, and I will give you rest." (Matthew 11:28).

I prayed every day telling the Lord, I would give Him until Tuesday, 22 May 2018, "for them to get back to me." If they didn't, I would know I wasn't successful in securing the job. To my delight, on Tuesday, 22 May 2018, I received a call from the organisation congratulating me on my successful application and recommending that I start the following Monday with a seven-day induction. This was to be a permanent part-time position. The

Lord has a sense of humour, as this is one field I said I didn't want to work in. I am still currently working in this field.

The Lord fulfilled His promise when He said He would bless three people with a job and, the following month, four people with jobs. Prayer is powerful; God hears every word we say. God will deliver as He tells us if we ask with a sincere and contrite heart. "Whatever you ask in my name, I will do it, that the Father may be glorified in the Son; if you ask anything in my name, I will do it." (John 14:13-14).

Don't be impatient or think that God hasn't heard your prayers if He doesn't answer immediately. He always hears our prayers. If God does not give us what we pray for, take it as a sign that it is not meant for us. He may have a better plan in place for you. If anyone knows you, it is God who knitted you together in your mother's womb. His timing is always perfect and in our best interest. Trust God completely, allowing Him to take the wheel. Let go of the old and let God breathe new life into new situations.

Chapter 10

When Few Gather, God Still Moves

In 2017, the Spirituality Commission Group decided to hold a Lenten Retreat in our parish. We decided to ask Fr. Rony VC if he would be available to conduct the retreat for our parish. He agreed, and so we began planning for the retreat.

We organised flyers to advertise in the various parishes in the surrounding neighbourhoods. So, a friend and I drove around, asking the different parishes if we could place the flyers on their noticeboards.

About two weeks before the retreat began, I had a disturbing dream, and when I woke up in the morning, I felt confused. In the dream, I saw a small chapel where about forty people were sitting in the pews, while a priest dressed in liturgical vestments stood in the sanctuary speaking to them. This troubled me because the Lord seemed to tell me that only a few would attend the retreat. We had done a lot of advertising in our parish and neighbouring parishes, so we were expecting more than forty people.

On the day of the retreat, Fr. Rony George VC arrived with about four of his team members. I recall telling Fr. Rony about my dream, and he advised me not to worry and to leave it in God's hands.

When it was time to start the retreat, only a few people were there and a few more arrived shortly after we had began. About twenty minutes into the retreat, Fr. Rony was giving a talk from the lectern. After a while, he stepped away, stood at the bottom of the sanctuary, and said he didn't need a microphone since there were only a few people; he preferred to stand below the steps of the sanctuary. Although the attendance was around forty, it was an excellent Lenten Retreat. Everyone felt the same. It was intimate, spiritual, and uplifting, with a powerful message.

I invited Fr. Roni and his team to our house for dinner, and he mentioned it was a good retreat and he enjoyed it. The number isn't important. God chose us individually to be in His presence, spending those precious hours with Him. God clearly showed me the number to expect. I was nervous and secretly hoped that the dream wouldn't come true. In the end, it was God's providence that prevailed.

When God Orchestrates the Journey

One Friday afternoon, I received an email from a member of our Spirituality Group. The email stated that she was requesting my contact details. She explained to this team member that I do Bible Study and have connections with the Divine Retreat Centre. This lady asked if I was going to the Divine Retreat Centre on Sunday, and what time I would be leaving. I replied yes and asked if she would like a lift. She replied, "She was grateful as she didn't like driving far." She then mentioned that her sister would also like to attend the Retreat. I replied, telling her there would also be a place for her sister. She thanked me and called me an angel.

I had no idea who I was corresponding with, but she knew me. I didn't recognise her name, but I was trying to recall if I knew her, and then a face came to me. I knew the face but didn't recognise the name. I realised that the Lord revealed the person to me. When I picked her up, it was the same face I had seen. I told her what had happened and how the Lord revealed her face to me. She often comes to our parish, and I see her at Mass.

On our way to the Retreat Centre, she told me that at the Lenten Retreat held at our parish the previous month, she had placed a petition in the box, and her prayer request had been answered. She wanted to thank God for answering her prayers. She had placed the petition for her sister's husband in the box, so her sister also wanted to express her gratitude to God.

She told me she couldn't send any emails on Friday, but only mine was successful. She then mentioned she was considering whom to ask about going to the Divine Retreat Centre, and suddenly, she thought of me. She told her sister that I had offered to take her without asking me, and she was so taken aback that she realised the Lord was making all these arrangements possible. This was the first time they would be attending the Divine Retreat Centre.

When God invites you to his place of worship, no matter how far it is, he will make all the arrangements for you so you can be there. He always sends someone to help you if He knows there will be obstacles in your path. He will plan everything perfectly and get you where you need to be. Do you trust God and have enough faith, as small as a mustard seed, to allow God to take control of your life and be there for you when you are experiencing difficulties? Do you believe in the Power of God?

Everything turned out very well for this lady and her sister. We both agreed that the Almighty Hand of God was upon us in this situation. God is all powerful and will always answer your prayers, especially when you surrender everything into His hands and believe that nothing is impossible when you pray and seek God's help. He will always answer, but in His time.

A Parking Dilemma and God's Perfect Timing

I was rostered to help on Saturday and Sunday during one of the weekend retreats in 2018. The retreat was fully booked, so I stayed at a Motel in Gosford. I had no desire to drive back home late at night on my own and then have to return early in the morning.

On Sunday morning, I had to be at the Retreat Centre by 7:00 a.m. to help set the tables for breakfast, which is served at 7:45

a.m. When it was time to leave at 6:40 a.m., I couldn't get out of the parking lot because I couldn't reverse out of the parking bay. The car parked beside me was remarkably close to mine, leaving me little room to manoeuvre. The small car park, with a brick wall behind me, made reversing out of the parking bay quite difficult.

It was still very early, and since it was a Sunday morning, hardly anyone was about.

I couldn't return to the room because I had already put the keys in the lockbox, which is used for those wanting to leave early. I hoped to find someone to either take my car out or guide me from the parking bay. I prayed, asking Jesus to send me an Angel to help me. While waiting, I felt inspired to pray the Rosary.

Within 10 minutes of finishing the Rosary, I noticed a man walking towards his car. I immediately jumped out of my car, approached him, and asked if he could help me reverse out of the parking bay, as I was having difficulty doing so. He offered to help but he didn't drive my car. He guided me, and after several manoeuvres, I finally managed to drive out. He also agreed that the space was quite tight for me to use. I thanked him and drove off.

As I was driving back to the Retreat Centre, I burst into tears, overwhelmed by the realisation that the Lord had sent someone — an Angel — to help me. Without His assistance, I would have sat there much longer. I couldn't stop myself from thanking and praising Our Lord for sending an Angel at the perfect time when I needed help, even though I first had to recite the Rosary.

The Lord is kind, merciful, slow to anger, and rich in Mercy. I managed to get back to the Retreat Centre with plenty of time to spare.

Chapter 11

Parousia and the Message I Couldn't Ignore

One of my ministries in the parish is serving as an Extraordinary Eucharistic Minister. I also administer Communion to the sick who are housebound in our parish and the sick in the hospital. When I visit the sick, I usually receive the Eucharist in my Pyx from the presiding priest at that Mass.

They would then say a prayer for the sick we were visiting. One Sunday morning, I didn't take the Eucharist from our parish, so after Mass ended, I went straight to the hospital, where a chapel housed a Tabernacle. As I opened the Tabernacle and the curtain, I felt so overwhelmed that tears streamed down my cheeks. I instantly felt the real presence of the Lord surround me. It felt like I was taken back in time when I recalled these words, "(...) and the curtain of the temple was torn in two. Then Jesus, crying with a loud voice, said," Father, into your hands I commit my Spirit! And having said this, he breathed his last." (Luke 23:45-46).

It felt as though I was entering the Holy of Holies. This was my first experience of opening a Tabernacle. After that beautiful moment, I was so mindful of what I was doing that I treated each host as gently as possible while holding the precious body of Christ in my hands as I administered the Eucharist to the patients that morning.

One Sunday afternoon on the 17th of November 2019, after administering Communion to the sick at Nepean Hospital and heading home, the Spirit of the Lord placed the word Parousia upon my heart. It was so vivid that it momentarily shook me. I kept repeating the word until I arrived home, trying to understand its significance. I remember the specific spot where this happened.

Our parish holds a Bible study once a year, lasting about three months, depending on the book of the Bible we're studying. We ordered the books through Parousia Media, which was the first time I've encountered the word Parousia. Our Spirituality Commission group, of which I'm a member, organises the Bible study annually. Due to COVID-19, we were unable to hold any Bible studies in 2020-2021. We resumed Bible study in 2023.

On Monday afternoon, when I got home from work, I called Parousia Media, to ask if they are a publishing, Company. The lady I spoke with said no, they only do print media. I kept asking her to see if there was a connection to the word Parousia which the Spirit of the Lord gave me. I wanted to find out if the Lord wanted me to use them to publish this book. Eventually I told her how I received the word Parousia. She was a lovely lady and very patient with me. She advised me to pray about it and ask God to help me discern what He wants me to do.

About nine months earlier, at one of the Last Sunday Retreats at the Retreat Centre in Somersby, the founder and owner of Parousia Media and his family gave a beautiful testimony of how God inspired him to start his business.

During the COVID-19 lockdown in Sydney, we had to watch Mass online. On Sunday mornings, I would get up as if I were going to Mass at our parish. I still fasted and dressed for the Mass. I never watched it on television because I didn't want to feel like I was watching a TV programme. Instead, I used my phone and sat at my prayer table, with the candles lit. I made my surroundings prayerful. This was my way of feeling spiritually connected, and it made me feel as if I was participating in the Mass.

One evening after work, I watched a weekday Mass on TV, celebrated by Fr. Michael Payyapilly VC. To my surprise, he spoke about Parousia and explained what it meant. It is the second coming of Christ. I was surprised; I had no idea what it meant at the time, and it never occurred to me to look it up online. A few months later, during Fr. Rony George's talk at one of the last Sunday Retreats, he also mentioned Parousia and explained its meaning, referring to the second coming. I had a sense the Lord was trying to tell me something.

The Lord delivered this message to me, and He knew I was unsure of its meaning. He used His shepherds to explain it to me, not once but twice. As Christians, we have read in the Bible and believe in his return on the last day, yet nobody knows the hour.

Only the Father knows. We should live our daily lives as if He were returning today; therefore, we should live in peace and harmony, forgive those who have offended us, and love one another as God loves us —-He sacrificed His only Son for us. When you look at the cross, may it remind you of God's enduring love for us.

"For God so loved the world that He gave his only-begotten Son, that whoever believes in him should not perish but have eternal life." (John 3:16). We must repent of our sinful ways and return to God. We should follow the two greatest commandments Jesus gave us: (...) "You shall love the Lord your God with all your heart, and with all your soul, and with all your mind. (...) And a second is like it, you shall love your neighbour as yourself". (Matthew 22:37,39).

Love remains the central theme here. It's not easy to love someone who persecutes you, nor is it easy to forgive them. "Jesus tells us to forgive seventy times seven." How can we expect God to forgive us if we struggle to forgive our brothers and sisters in Christ? When you forgive, you find a new sense of freedom. It's worthwhile to reflect on the Ten Commandments, as this is how God expects us to live our lives. While the Israelites wandered in the desert for forty years, they were disobedient in God's eyes, and He was not pleased with them. Therefore, He introduced the Ten Commandments, to guide them towards a more righteous life. The Ten Commandments are God's law, which He intended us to follow. Reflecting on these Commandments is beneficial, as it will help you see where you can improve and live a life pleasing to God.

Parousia - We must be ready for this day, His Second coming.

Chapter 12

Unexpected Guests and God's Perfect Plan

This is a story of how the Lord inspires us, often without us realising it. In 2015, on a Good Friday morning, I cooked dinner for our return from the Good Friday Service. I was preparing dinner for four adults, but little did I know that the Lord had His plans.

I had cooked several dishes that day, which was unusual, because I usually prepare two fish meals for dinner on Good Friday. My daughter decided she wanted hot chips with her fried fish. I wasn't keen on the idea, since there was plenty of food, but I eventually let her go ahead. Only later did I realise the significance of this seemingly simple decision in the "Grand Plan of God." It was a part of His perfect plan, guiding our actions and decisions, even in the smallest matters.

While they were out buying the hot chips, they ran into our parish priest, Fr. Brian OSA, who was looking for a place to buy fish for dinner. They told him everything was closed, because it was Good Friday. When they returned home, my daughter's fiancé (at the time) told me what had happened.

I was saddened to hear that our parish priest wouldn't be having a proper dinner that night. So, I asked my daughter's fiancé to call and invite him to join us for dinner. However, he felt too embarrassed to do so. Instead, I found our parish priest's number in the parish news bulletin and rang him to extend the dinner invitation. He sounded surprised to hear my voice, so I explained that he had spoken to my daughter and her fiancé earlier. Because my daughter's fiancé had a close connection with Fr. Brian through his involvement in the parish youth group and with the Augustinian Volunteers Australia, I suggested he should be the one to contact our parish priest. After I convinced him to join us, he agreed and thanked me for the invitation.

About 10 minutes later, he called to say he couldn't accept the invitation because he had two Brothers staying with him. I assured him it wouldn't be a problem as I had cooked plenty of food. I eventually convinced him that he wouldn't be able to buy any fish for dinner and that I had plenty of food for everyone to eat.

He eventually accepted my invitation. As we were having dinner, I realised that God had planned everything perfectly. The timing was perfect; had there been one minute out, they would have missed each other. When I was cooking so much food, I had no idea that morning that we would sit down with his Shepherds later that evening.

That day I felt a little guilty, because I had no connection with our parish priest. I never really got to know him. It was a good morning, and at the end of the Mass, I said thank you, Father. This was well before I became actively involved in our parish. When I looked around the table that day, I saw five nationalities come together to share a meal on Good Friday. There was plenty of food to serve seven adults, and there was plenty left over. We agreed without a doubt that the Lord had planned everything so perfectly that day.

After that Good Friday dinner, I felt in my heart that the Lord was speaking to me about his shepherds, so I invited the priest over for a meal on Good Friday or at least once during the year. If I couldn't have a priest in my home for a meal, I would cook and take it to the Retreat Centre or try to take them out for lunch or dinner. Due to their busy schedules, it happened less often than I would have liked.

I also felt a calling to pray for all priests, and I have honoured this calling. To this day, I continue to pray for priests and for more vocations to the priesthood and religious life. I have come to know many priests, and some of them consistently offer me spiritual guidance. Please pray for all priests so that, by the grace of God, they remain faithful servants of the Lord and always serve as a light to others in darkness.

Chapter 13

The Power of Prayer in God's Perfect Plan

As we continued attending retreats, my life began to change. My heart was beginning to be cleansed and renewed. Like flowers, they wither and die when the roots are dry. They must be watered and nourished to survive and flourish again. My life felt the same.

To survive spiritually, I needed to be nourished with the Word of God, allowing my heart to grow and flourish, and to open my eyes, ears, and heart to hear it. By reading and listening to the Word of God daily, or as often as possible, you will begin to change. You will realise that God is a loving, merciful, and forgiving God. You must be rooted in God's Word for change to happen.

I met a lady at the retreats, and as we chatted, she asked about my children and discovered I was a grandmother. After attending retreats for a good couple of months, she asked me to pray for her daughter to have a baby, as she was struggling to conceive and longed to be a grandmother. She had tears in her eyes when she asked, and I remember feeling very saddened for her as I looked into her eyes.

She desperately wanted her daughter to experience motherhood and have her own child. As they say, a mother's love is unconditional. It wasn't about her wanting to become a grandmother, but for her daughter to be blessed with a child.

Only she knew what she was going through. I didn't question anything, as there was no need to know all the details. I offered to pray for her daughter to be blessed with a child and I was genuinely sincere in my response.

At the time, I believed she had asked a few people to pray for her daughter. I always included her daughter in my prayers. One day, I had a dream that her daughter was pregnant. In the dream, I saw a little girl. When I woke that morning, I remembered everything from my dream. I told my husband, so I knew then that the lady's daughter would become pregnant and have a girl. I never got to meet her daughter.

When I saw the lady again, I reassured her not to worry because her daughter would become pregnant and have a baby girl. I believed and had faith that Jesus was revealing this to me. She was happy but also anxious when I told her. I didn't see her for a couple of months after that.

We were both at a Last Sunday Retreat long after that. I hadn't seen her all morning, but during the lunch break, she found me and called me aside because she wanted to talk. She told me that her daughter had a baby girl. I was so excited to hear the news; I jumped for joy. I thanked and praised our Lord Jesus Christ for answering our prayers. I said to her, "The dream. I told you it would happen, and that your daughter would have a baby girl."

She told me that morning she didn't want to attend the retreat, but something kept nudging her to go, so she did. Now, I felt similar. I had a lot on that weekend, so I decided not to go to the Sunday retreat. That was until I received a phone call from a lady asking if I would be going to the retreat on Sunday and if I could give her a lift. I heard myself saying to her, "If you want to go, I am happy for you to come with me."

I surprised myself and realised what I had just said, but it was too late to retract my answer. I had given her a lift a few times before, so I knew she would have missed spending the day with the Lord if I hadn't taken her. Late Saturday evening, her husband called me to say that his wife couldn't attend because something unexpected had come up. I could have chosen not to attend the Last Sunday Retreat, but since I was already prepared to go, I realised that the Lord had planned it, as He knew I had no intention of going. God had a reason for wanting me there, so my husband and I decided to go.

I knew God had planned everything. Although I didn't want to attend the retreat, my inner voice prompted me to go. I wouldn't have heard the great news about the baby had I not gone.

I hadn't seen her again for a remarkably long time. It was about 18 months later when I saw her again. She shared some great news: her daughter was pregnant once more. I then asked her if she had asked a few people to pray for her daughter during her first pregnancy, and to my surprise, she said no. I was the only one she had asked to pray. I was taken aback, as I assumed she had asked a few grandmothers to pray for her and her daughter. God plans everything to perfection. When we pray, Jesus tells us, "Therefore I tell you, whatever you ask in prayer, believe that you receive it, and you will." (Mark 11:24).

A Dream, a Baby Girl, and Facing My Giant

My youngest daughter was planning to have her first child. She faced some medical issues, which meant she might not be able to fall pregnant. She was under specialist care and was advised she could start planning to have her first child. I began praying for her to be healed and for her to be blessed with a family.

My daughter and son-in-law live in a two-storey house. One night, I had a vivid dream that my daughter was pregnant, and in the dream, she gave birth to a baby girl. I was at their place, carrying the baby, as we went down the stairs. I had already reached the middle of the stairs in the dream. Due to a previous knee injury, I didn't enjoy climbing stairs. I felt anxious when I realised I would have to walk up and down the steps with the baby. The Lord assured me I would manage climbing the stairs with the baby; it was my giant, and God would heal my fears.

My knee injury happened about two weeks before I was scheduled to leave on my first Pilgrimage to the Holy Land in 2016. I was devastated because I knew the chances of making the trip were slim. I struggled to walk, and climbing stairs was even harder.

My doctor referred me to a Physiotherapist, and I explained that I was due to travel soon, which would involve a lot of walking and stair climbing. He treated me and helped me get ready to walk and climb a few stairs without much trouble. I was relieved to know I would be able to fulfil my dream of being a pilgrim in the Holy Land. All glory to God for enabling me to accomplish this.

I knew God was revealing that my daughter would have a baby girl. When she revealed to us that she was pregnant, I was ecstatic. Although I knew she would fall pregnant and have a baby girl, I was still surprised.

One day, she invited my husband and me over to their place. When we arrived, after a few minutes, she gave us a gift and told me to close my eyes and take it out. It was a teddy bear with a top on it. Still with my eyes l closed, I said it was a girl, and I opened my eyes to see the teddy bear wearing a pink top with the words "It's a girl."

I was thrilled to hear that she was going to have a daughter. I told her, 'I knew, and God revealed it to me in a dream.' God is so great; all praise and thanks be to Him. Children are truly a blessing from God.

Seeing the I AM in Everyday Moments

One day, I decided to bake a cake and ice it with a thin glacé icing using a zig-zag motion. When the icing had set, I noticed three letters had formed that I hadn't deliberately written. At first, I thought it was my imagination, but then I got a second opinion when my daughter's fiancé visited. I asked him to tell me what he saw on the cake; he read out the same letters without knowing what I was seeing. When my eldest daughter came home, I asked her to tell me what she saw on the cake. She also read out the same letters. We all saw the same letters that were written on the cake.

Before I started cooking and baking, I asked the Lord to bless my hands and the food I was preparing for His shepherds. The words are, I AM. I was surprised because I was undertaking a Bible study at the time and studying the book of Exodus. During that week, for homework, we had to read and answer questions based on Exodus 1-18. God revealed His name to Moses as "I AM who I AM" (3:14). I spoke to my husband about the name, and we discussed what I had read in the Bible.

Before I volunteered at the Divine Retreat Centre, I was asked to help at the Inauguration on 24 April 2016. I guided people into the premises and directed them to their respective locations for the retreat and the Inauguration of the Retreat Centre.

One of the volunteers came to relieve me as I was needed elsewhere. At one point, I was sitting in a room helping the ladies, with a few men supporting us. Then, I heard the whisper of the Holy Spirit, drawing my attention to someone in the room wearing a waistcoat. I looked at the person in the waistcoat but was unsure of what I was searching for. I couldn't see the back of the waistcoat, so I continued with the task at hand. I heard another whisper urging me to look, and by then, the person had turned their back to me. I was able to read on the back of his waistcoat the following:

"I BELIEVE in the GREAT I AM," and at the bottom of the letters was written Exodus 3:14. I was in awe, firstly because I don't believe in coincidence; Luke 1:37 tells us, "For with God nothing is impossible." He times everything to perfection. I heard the whisper of the Holy Spirit telling me to look at the person wearing the waistcoat. Secondly, the words I AM were the exact words written on the cake a few weeks before the day of the inauguration.

The waistcoats were designed for the volunteers to wear for the Inauguration weekend of the Divine Retreat Centre, Somersby.

Chapter 14

How God's Whisper Became a Book

In 2015, I attended a weekend retreat at the Divine Retreat Centre on Lutana Road, Somersby. During Adoration, Fr. Michael Payyapilly VC said, "Someone will write a book for God." I remember looking around to see who it could be. I never thought for one minute that I could author a book. I was broken when I first started attending retreats, and Praising and Worshipping God in a Charismatic way was new to me. After that retreat, I never thought about it again.

Faith

What is Faith? – St Augustine of Hippo explains it so beautifully.

> **"It is to believe what you do not see; the reward of this faith is to see what you believe."**

When I first heard the Spirit of the Lord speak about writing the book, I felt a mixture of nervousness, fear, awe, trembling, and confusion. I knew what I heard was not a figment of my imagination; the message was clear. I doubted myself, as I was just an ordinary person trying to live my life according to the teachings of Christ, which was not easy. Along our journey, we stumble many times, and our cross can become too heavy to carry, which is not what God intended for us. When we fall, we should ask God to give us the strength and grace to lift ourselves up and keep walking towards the narrow door.

I have written this book through my faith and belief in God because I feel His presence around me each time I write. Therefore, I know God is with me and guiding me throughout my writing. It is only through my faith that I can succeed. The fruits of my faith are to believe and trust that God has called me to author this book and that He will help me. I also trust in His divine providence, and the reward is to see it completed.

"To obey (from the Latin *ob-audire* ", to hear or listen to") in faith is to submit freely to the word that has been heard because its truth is guaranteed by God, who is Truth himself. Abraham is the model of such obedience offered us by Sacred Scripture. The

Virgin Mary is its most perfect embodiment." (Catechism of the Catholic Church's second edition – 144).

My prayer is that this book will inspire those who have lost faith, hope and trust in God, and are struggling emotionally, financially, physically, or spiritually. May they come to believe and know that God sees and understands everything you are going through. He loves you as He knitted you in your mother's womb. He knows the perfect time to send His angels to help you.

Don't lose faith and hope; give God time to guide the right people to help you. He will never leave you desolate. Look to God and be radiant, and He will help you. God is always working in the background; He never sleeps. He knows what each of us needs. Pray without ceasing, and do not lose faith and hope. I have obeyed God's calling to complete this book, so that others who doubt and have lost hope, faith, and trust in God may return to Him, and that you may find the inner peace, love, mercy, and forgiveness that only He can provide.

"Have no anxiety about anything, but in everything, by prayer and supplication with thanksgiving, let your request be known to God". (Philippians 4:6).

This book was written in response to an inspiration I received on Tuesday morning, August 6, 2019, while driving to work. The Spirit of the Lord inspired me to write a book titled "A Woman of Faith." I remember the exact spot where the Spirit of God spoke to me. My heart was racing, and I was shaking. I felt uncomfortable with the title because I felt as though I was being too proud of myself and my faith. The letter {A} troubled me, singling me out as one person. I was restless all day because the book wasn't supposed to be about me. It should be about God and what He has done for me. I pondered this all day and wanted to change the title, but then I realised I did not choose the title; God inspired me to do so.

I began praying fervently, asking God for validation on whether He wanted me to author a book and to clarify the title that day. I felt restless all day and needed to know if what I heard was true. The next day, Wednesday the 7th of August 2019, during our family prayer night, as the Gospel was read from Matthew 15:21-28, I followed along in my Bible.

While reading, I felt inspired to glance at the sub-heading in the next column on the same page, which read "The Canaanite Woman's Faith." When I saw that, I started trembling and my heart began racing. God confirmed what I longed to know. Although I still felt uneasy about the book title, I began calling it Woman of Faith, as I felt a bit more at ease with this name. I found the title difficult because, out of all the words in the dictionary, this is the only word I struggle to say in public, and that is 'woman'. I wondered how I could tell people the title of the book. So, believe me when I say that I didn't come up with the name for the book.

On the 8th of August 2019, during Bible Study, we discussed Sacred Scripture in the Catechism of the Catholic Church 105-108, especially 106, which states that:

"God inspired the human authors of the sacred books. To compose the sacred books, God chose certain men who, all the while he employed them in this task, made full use of their own faculties and powers so that, though he acted in them and by them, it was by them, it was as true authors that they consigned to writing whatever he wanted written and no more." (CCC 106)

My heart was on fire, and I was in awe. I knew God was answering my prayers and trying to get my attention by telling me He wants me to write the book and that He is the author.

On 10 October 2019, I prayed for inspiration and guidance to write the book and asked Jesus to send the Holy Spirit upon me. I then decided to read God's Word 2019 for the daily reading. It was Perseverance in Prayer: "(...) v13If you then, who are evil, know how to give good gifts to your children, how much more will the heavenly Father give the Holy Spirit to those who ask him!" (Luke 11:5-13).

I've always felt inclined to write down significant moments as they happened to me. I consistently recorded the date and time. I never understood why I did this, but at the same time, the Spirit of the Lord inspired me to do so. This was before I felt the Spirit of the Lord inspiring me to write a book. All dates mentioned in this book are accurate records of the time, date, and place where they occurred.

I was scared to do anything that wasn't pleasing to God. I didn't believe in myself or think I was capable of doing what God asked of me. I needed to be strong in my faith, because I didn't feel worthy enough to carry out God's plans for me.

I went for spiritual counselling, and Fr. Roni George VC confirmed that God wants me to write this book. By then I had already started some of the writing. This was the validation I needed to continue with my writing. After writing intermittently for a few months, I stopped altogether. I began to doubt whether God truly wanted me to write a book. I felt like Thomas, who doubted that Jesus had risen until Jesus appeared in the room and told him to put his fingers in his side. Only then did Thomas believe.

When God asks you to do something for Him, He will make His message clear and often use others to deliver it. While having breakfast, I noticed that in the mornings, someone on television would be interviewed about a book they had just published. This happened several times over a few years.

As I was nearing the end of my writing, I realised that several times in the morning on television, while having breakfast, they were interviewing people who wrote memoirs, which I am also working on. I saw this as another sign for me to finish the book. I noticed that the timing was always perfect.

I realised that this was no coincidence, as God times everything to perfection. Around this time, many people were publishing books. An author who was being interviewed was asked," How do you go about writing a book?" "He replied ", Just sit down and start writing." It was easier said than done. It took me about another six months before I started writing again. After a few weeks, I developed writer's block. I still didn't want to accept that God called me to author this book. I did not believe in myself.

I don't watch much television, as I prefer to watch inspirational talks or Christian movies on YouTube or on the Christian channels on Television. One day, I put on the YouTube Channel, and on the homepage, there was a video by Fr. Antony Parankimalil VC, titled 'How to Discern God's Voice.' I watched the whole talk and realised that I could relate to everything he said. I wrote everything down so I could remember it for later use. This is what he said:

"God speaks to us through the Word of God, the Holy Spirit, through other people, utterances, voices, angels, dreams, visions, and specific circumstances or situations." I have experienced most of these.

He then explained how to discern if it is from God. "It has to be rooted and based on the Word of God. It should be based on the teachings of the Catholic Church, help you to do new things in your life, and never forget this incident that has taken place."

While listening to him, I realised that everything he said had already happened to me. I remember the visions very clearly, the exact spot on the road where I heard the Spirit of God speaking to me, the dreams, and the voice of God, as if it were yesterday. When God wants your attention, He sometimes acts in unusual ways. This was no coincidence; God plans everything perfectly, and His timing is impeccable. When you ignore God's calling, He will speak to you louder until you do what He is asking you to do. You cannot run and hide; He will find you.

To boost my self-confidence, I decided to enrol in a short writing course. I found a college that offered weekend classes, which would make attending easier since I was working during the week. I managed to find a college about a 35-minute drive from my home. I enrolled and paid for the course, excited that it would give me the confidence I needed. It was on Saturdays, so I knew I would be able to attend. A few days before it was scheduled to start, I received a call from the college advising me that the course had been cancelled due to insufficient enrolment.

I was devastated, because I had been looking forward to learning how to write. I was refunded my money and asked if I would like to stay on the list for the next semester. I gladly agreed. The following semester arrived, so I enrolled again and made my payment. A few days before the class was scheduled to start, I received a phone call informing me that there were not enough students and the class had to be cancelled.

Once again, I was devastated. I asked the lady if I could enrol in any other courses, and she said no, as there were none in the field of Writing at the time. I was so disappointed, but then I realised that it was not God's plan for me to do the course, as He was going to help me, being the author. When something is not in your best interest, He will put blockages in the way. God wanted me to trust Him, have faith, and believe He would help me, as He is the author.

I needed to find a way to have the vision I saw in the Holy Land painted. I didn't realise how many pictures there were when I searched for a picture of Jesus' face. I chose one and kept looking in case another resembled it even more. Eventually, I selected two more images. I was happy with my choices. Then I realised the three pictures were identical to the Shroud of Turin. Next, I had to find specific mountains that resembled what I had seen in the vision. Luckily, I found mountains almost identical to those in my vision. Finally, I tried to combine the three images into a single picture.

The next challenge was finding an artist to bring the vision to life, so I turned to God, asking for help to select someone. I work in Aged Care as a Care Worker, a role that involves visiting clients in their homes. Around this time, I pondered how to find someone to paint the vision. In several homes I visited, I noticed beautiful paintings on the walls. When I asked who created the paintings, they told me they had. However, due to their age, they no longer paint.

One day, I had to visit a client who wasn't one of my regulars, because her usual carer was off work that day. In her kitchen, I noticed a picture of the Sacred Heart of Jesus on her fridge. I paused to look at it and said a little prayer. Something stirred within me as I offered that prayer. When I entered the lounge where the client was sitting, I took a seat and we started talking. I noticed some paintings on the wall and commented on how beautiful they were. To my surprise, she told me she had painted them. They were stunning. She also told me that she paints and was in the process of finishing a painting for someone.

I confidently told her that I had been looking for someone to paint an image for me. She was the first person I confided in about this. While speaking with her, the Spirit of God prompted me to ask her to do the painting. So, I inquired if she wanted to paint an image I had seen. I explained that it was a very private matter and asked her not to share what I revealed with anyone. I told her about the vision I wanted painted, and she said she would love to paint it. I was so excited, that I mentioned seeing the picture of the Sacred Heart of Jesus on the fridge. When I said a prayer, I felt the Spirit of God stir within me.

I then told her I knew; God was revealing to me that you are the one He has chosen. She was just as excited as I was. When I visited her during work hours, I explained that I needed to get permission from my manager to decide whether she would be allowed to paint the vision for me.

I contacted my manager and asked if I could meet with her, so she scheduled a time for us to catch up. During the meeting, I explained that I had asked a client if she could paint a picture for me. She asked if I would pay her, and I said yes. I didn't tell her what the painting was about. She responded, "Because it was not my regular client and it was only a fill-in for someone, she could go ahead and do the painting for me." I was so overwhelmed to the point of tears as I hadn't expected such a positive outcome. She asked why I was crying, and I replied that I was happy because the painting meant a lot to me and that you have agreed, allowing the client to paint for me.

I could hardly believe what I heard, as the organisation's policies are very strict regarding carer-client relationships outside of working hours. I was eager to share this good news with the client. Is God not great? His planning is perfectly executed. He found the artist and arranged for me to visit her home. She was thrilled when I told her she had permission to proceed with the painting. The artist had faced significant family issues and had temporarily stopped painting. We were both experiencing blockages, and I paused my writing for quite some time. God will rearrange your schedule so that you find yourself in the right place at the right time, and He must also adjust someone else's schedule to fulfil His plans for you. God orchestrates everything perfectly; nothing is a coincidence when God is at work.

"I will instruct you and teach you the way you should go; I will counsel you with my eye upon you." (Psalm 32:8)

I asked the artist not to disclose the details of the painting to anyone, as I wanted to keep it sacred and not share my intentions for the book with anyone. I confided in our parish priest, the Spiritual Director, Fr. Roni at the Retreat Centre, and a friend, as I wanted only a few people to know.

At the same time, I was protective of God's calling. It's a spiritual book, and I didn't want any negative comments about my trust, faith, and belief that God had called me to do this for Him. I needed to have faith and trust in God to complete this task. I didn't want anyone asking when I would finish the book, as I had no idea. That would have added pressure. I had to keep faith and trust in God so that when He was ready, He would let me know. Another reason was that if it never got published, only a few people would know, and I wouldn't have to answer questions about what happened to the book.

I know I must complete this book soon, because the Holy Spirit inspires me to do so.

Chapter 15

A stranger's card and a silent message

I continued to pray and ask God to confirm whether He wanted me to write this book. St Anthony is one of my favourite Saints, so I prayed and asked God to send St Anthony to me, preferably in a dream.

On Sunday, 18th August 2019, after the Sunday morning Mass, I visited Nepean Hospital in Penrith to administer Communion to the sick. I was scheduled to go once a month. As I approached a patient on my roster, he was sitting on his bed with a card in his hand, waiting for me to arrive. I introduced myself to him. He extended his hand and, without saying anything, handed me the card to look at. The lighting around his bedside was dim, so I couldn't read the card. I put on my reading glasses, and when I saw the card, I was shocked and speechless. I was holding a prayer card to St Anthony.

He told me he prays to St Anthony every day. Once again, God heard my prayer and responded. He responded in such a way that St. Anthony was not in a dream; he used this patient in the hospital to confirm my doubts about writing the book. My issue was that I didn't believe in myself and didn't feel worthy of being chosen by God to write a book for Him.

On Monday, 19th August 2019, I prayed and asked God for further validation about writing the book and to speak to me through His Word. I opened the Bible to (v27) "Jesus looked at them and said, 'With men it is impossible, but not with God; for all things are possible with God'". (Mark 10 :13- 31).

After reading the Bible, I felt inspired to read the day's gospel reading. I opened the book God's Word 2019, and part of the passage I had just read was Matthew 19:16-22.

Long before I was inspired to write this book, I was inspired to fast. Therefore, I would fast on Fridays. I would eat breakfast, drink water during the day, and have fish for dinner, as I abstained from red meat. A few years later, while attending a retreat with visiting priest Fr. Mathew from India at St Agatha's Catholic Church in Pennant Hills, I felt inspired by the Holy Spirit to fast on Wednesdays, and I felt this conviction quite strongly.

The Blessed Mother has asked us to pray and fast on Wednesdays and Fridays. Since then, I fasted every Wednesday and Friday. However, I no longer fast these days due to health-related issues. Instead, I have made a personal sacrifice by eating light meals on Wednesdays and Fridays, abstaining from all forms of flesh, and only eating vegetarian meals on Wednesdays. On Fridays I continue to eat only fish.

On Wednesday, 23 October 2019, I ended my fast with prayer, including a plea for God to confirm whether He was prompting me to write this book and to offer guidance and inspiration. I also prayed for Ann, asking the Lord to bless her and her hands whenever she attempted to paint the vision. I understood my request was challenging, but I believed God had chosen her. During this time, she was dealing with personal issues, and her husband fell ill. A few months later, she became unwell and faced a period of struggle. The painting project came to a complete halt. I had to hold onto faith that everything would unfold as intended and that the painting of the vision would ultimately be completed.

I then prayed and asked God to speak to me through His word. After praying, I opened my Bible, and it opened to,

"God's reply. And the Lord answered me: Write the vision; make it plain upon tablets so he may run who reads it. For still, the vision awaits its time; it hastens to the end-it will not lie. If it seems slow wait for it; it will surely come, it will not delay." (Habakkuk 2: 2 – 4).

This reading provided the reassurance I needed regarding the vision Ann was painting. It has been a prolonged process, but I trust that God will keep His Word, and the vision will be revealed to everyone. As the reading states, it will not lie. I have provided an accurate description of the vision. God speaks to us through His Word. Whenever I seek clarification about anything, I always pray and open my Bible. God responds through His Holy Book because the Bible is the Word of God. (The painting of the vision is on the front cover of this book.)

A Statue, A Prayer, and an Unbelievable Discovery

My husband was asked to repair and repaint a statue of St Anthony for the Divine Retreat Centre. As the statue was in poor condition, I suggested buying a new one. He agreed, so I investigated purchasing a new statue of St Anthony.

Around this time, we both went on a weekend retreat. When I got back, I couldn't find my reading glasses. On the Monday after the retreat, I rang Fr. Michael Payyapilly VC to ask if he had seen them, but he hadn't come across them. I thought I'd left them in the room or on the couch where I sat before heading home. For weeks, I searched for them but couldn't find them anywhere. What started as weeks, escalated into months. I prayed to St Anthony, asking him to help me find my glasses. Luckily, I had an old pair that I could use in the meantime. I checked everywhere in my car, including in the boot. I use the boot about four times a week to put my shopping inside. Once, I bought a few bags of potting mix, some bags of garden soil, a few plants, and other heavy garden products and placed them in the boot.

I decided to look into buying a new statue of St Anthony. I rang Cardinal Newman Faith Resources at St Mary's and asked if they had any statues of St Anthony. This was a large statue, and I needed to ensure it was the correct one I was replacing. The manager told me she could order one for me. I mentioned I would bring the statue in to show her so I could be confident it was identical to the one that I had.

There was a small blanket in the boot of my car, so I spread it out and placed the statue on top. When I arrived at the shop, I took out the statue to show the lady I had spoken to on the phone. She told me she could order one for me, which would take about a week to arrive at her shop. After she examined it, I said I would take the statue back to my car as it was very fragile and heavy.

When I opened my boot, the first thing I saw on the blanket was my reading glasses. They weren't there when I placed the statue in the boot or took it out, as I would have definitely noticed them. I opened my boot several times while I was shopping throughout the week. I always put the shopping inside, but I never saw my glasses. I was so shocked and in disbelief, since I hadn't seen them when I placed the statue in the boot or when I took it out. I would have seen them or felt them when I straightened the blanket to lay the statue down.

St Anthony of Padua is one of my favourite saints. He is well known as the patron saint of lost articles. He has never let me down when I have prayed to him for help in finding anything I have lost. He always answers my prayers. I believe my glasses were misplaced for a reason, so a little miracle through St Anthony would happen. This also teaches me to persevere and have faith when praying. I asked the person who gave us the statue to repair and repaint it whether we could keep the old one, as it would be worthwhile to purchase a brand-new one. I now have the statue in my home. When I prayed for God to send me a message through St Anthony, God used a patient in the hospital to answer my prayers.

Chapter 16

When God's Plan Unfolds in Mysterious Ways

I have always tried to put the Corporal Works of Mercy into practice. In Matthew 25:35-45, Jesus speaks about feeding the hungry, visiting the sick, giving a drink to the thirsty, welcoming a stranger, clothing the naked, and visiting those in prison.

I volunteered for Vinnies for a few years but had to give up my membership because I needed to care for my grandson at that time. I didn't think it was fair on the other members, as I found home visits challenging. I have always enjoyed going out and helping those who are less fortunate. Their gratitude, humility, and the fact that we could assist someone in need were very rewarding. Seeing their faces light up with a smile when we left motivated me to stay involved with Vinnies for as long as I could.

For several years, until the COVID-19 pandemic, I would take communion to the sick in the hospital once a month on a Sunday morning. I found great fulfilment in this ministry, because all the patients I visited were always so grateful that we were called to it, as it allowed them to receive the Body of Christ on a Sunday Morning.

They were always eager to receive the Body of Christ, so most would be waiting for us to visit. Some would have tears in their eyes after receiving communion. I always carried out this ministry with the utmost reverence. Although a Chaplain was assigned to the hospital, he had to celebrate Sunday Mass at one of the parishes in the neighbouring suburbs.

I have welcomed strangers in various situations, both in groups and at home. One of my Ministries in the parish is a Welcomer. We greet everyone and make them feel welcome and part of the parish community. We must also ensure that all the assigned Ministers rostered for their ministries are present at Mass; otherwise, we must find a replacement for them. We are here to help anyone who needs assistance.

The one ministry I hadn't accomplished was visiting the prisons. I had felt this desire for several years, but it didn't eventuate into anything. I had no idea how to achieve this. I discussed this with my husband and my daughter, and both were opposed to the idea as they were worried about my safety. I prayed to God, asking for help so I could visit those in prison.

I am part of the RCIA Team (Rite of Christian Initiation of Adults), where we prepare adults seeking full Initiation into the Catholic Church at the Easter Vigil Mass. One of the team members from our RCIA Spiritual Journey was studying to become a Deacon, and one of his ministries included working in the Prisons.

One day, as we were leaving, he mentioned how busy he was with his role in the Prison Ministry. I then said I was interested in visiting the prisons but wasn't sure how to go about it. He asked if I'd like to come along, as they were organising a Closing Ceremony for those interested in the Prison Ministry. He said he would send me an email inviting me to the prison, and I would need to fill out the form and email it back to the contact person listed in the email.

I couldn't believe what I heard, so I kept asking him if that was all I needed to do, and he said yes. I also had to enter his name as the contact person who invited me. It was that straightforward.

After all that time spent pondering how I would accomplish this, I couldn't believe how easy it was. I was also in awe of how God planned everything so perfectly. It took me a while to understand what happened. God knew my heart and how passionate I felt about visiting those in prison. Everything just fell into place. God had answered my prayers in such a swift manner.

After a few days had passed, I told my husband and daughter I was going to visit a prison. They weren't pleased with the idea because they were worried about my safety. I assured them I would be safe, and this was an answer to my prayers.

The day arrived for me to visit the prison, and I experienced mixed emotions as I wasn't sure what to expect. The prison we visited was for minor offences. I felt at ease once we entered and passed through security, knowing that God was with us. When it was time for the inmates to arrive, we were asked to stand as they played a gospel song "When the Saints Come Marching In." There wasn't a dry eye in the room. We listened to their testimonies about how they had changed since coming to know God and realised that He is forgiving. Most of us had tears in our eyes just listening to their testimonies. An ex-prisoner shared his testimony, and once again, tears were shed by all. God can change even the most hardened hearts, and this is where healing begins.

My personal belief was that it was not my place to judge them, no matter what they did. They are still children of God, regardless of their past. I never thought I would encounter such a wonderful experience visiting a prison. The entire visit was both spiritually uplifting and awe-inspiring. I thank God for answering my prayers and giving me this awe-inspiring experience.

In 2024, I wanted to attend the Closing Ceremony again, but I wasn't sure when it would be held. Three weeks before the Closing Ceremony, I encountered the same person studying to become a Deacon. I hadn't seen him for a while, as he was no longer a team member of the RCIA journey. I had a similar experience when I spoke to him about the Prison Ministry during our first conversation.

When I asked about the next Closing Ceremony, he told me it would happen in three weeks. He sent me the invitation letter so I could submit my application. Once again, I was able to attend the Closing Ceremony. God graciously organised for us to meet at the church so I could arrange to attend the Closing Ceremony again.

God knew my heart's desire to attend the Closing Ceremony. With God, nothing is by chance. I had a beautiful experience and found it immensely powerful. Many tears were shed as we listened to testimonies on how the program made them realise that God is a loving, forgiving, and merciful God. Just watching them join in the hymns, which were so appropriately chosen for the ceremony, was fantastic. Listening to their testimonies and witnessing their desire to change is impressive; trusting God to lead them toward righteousness helps them establish a personal relationship with God. He will pour his mercy on anyone who seeks it.

God's hands are always outstretched towards us; all we have to do is grasp His hand and let God lead us along the path to holiness. God can transform the most hardened hearts. It is not our place to judge others. As Jesus told the people who wanted to stone the woman caught in adultery, (...)" Let him who is without sin among you be the first to throw a stone at her." (John 8:7).

No one is perfect, and we all deserve a second chance.

Chapter 17

A Divine Revelation Beyond Physical Bread

At the Divine Retreat Centre, we typically hold a volunteer retreat in January or February before the public retreats commence for the new year. The volunteers attended theirs from 10th to 12th January 2020. During that week, I felt prompted by the Holy Spirit to pray and read the Word of God. I spent some quiet time in prayer, then opened my Bible, and it fell open to Matthew 15:32-39, which tells the story of feeding the Four Thousand.

On Friday evening, we each received a sheet of paper with a few Bible references written on it for us to read and meditate on over the weekend. Each person was allocated different readings. I placed the paper in my bag and went to dinner. We were all allocated one hour, starting after dinner, to pray in front of the Blessed Sacrament. I had the first hour from 8:30 p.m. to 9:30 p.m.

After dinner, I headed to the Intercessory Chapel to pray and reached into my bag to find the paper with the Scripture readings. I couldn't find it anywhere. Somehow, I'd lost the sheet of paper between leaving the chapel and going for dinner. I knew that I had put it in my bag. With my Bible in hand, I prayed, asking God to reveal His Word to me. When I opened it, my eyes fell upon Matthew 15:32-39, The feeding of the Four Thousand. After reading, I took some time to reflect on the passage.

When I returned to my room after an hour in front of the Blessed Sacrament, I messaged Fr. Roni around 10:00 p.m. and told him that I had lost the paper with the readings he had given me. I asked if he could send them to me via text, which he did immediately. Before going to bed, I decided to choose one of the readings, and I opted the Gospel of Mark because it is known to be the shortest of the Gospels. The reading was Mark 8: 1-10, Feeding the Four Thousand.

When I decided to read Mark's Gospel, I had no idea what the reading would be, so I was surprised when I realised that it was the same passage, I had just read in the chapel about an hour earlier and two days before attending the Retreat. As I reflected on the reading, the connection to the Church and the Mass came to mind. This relates to the Eucharist, the bread that came down from Heaven, which helps sustain our Spiritual life when we receive the Eucharist during Mass. The Mass is the Highest form of Worship.

The Holy Spirit was enlightening me that the feeding of the Four Thousand was not about physically feeding people with food but about nourishing them spiritually through this book. On Sunday afternoon, we were asked to share our thoughts about the retreat and how it helped us grow spiritually in our ministry as volunteers. I spoke about the readings on "Feeding the Four Thousand" and what I believed God was trying to tell me, especially since I felt inspired to read this particular passage twice in a short period, at home, about two days before attending the retreat.

I explained that I knew what God was trying to tell me, but I couldn't reveal the meaning because I didn't want to disclose that I was in the process of drafting a book. A volunteer asked me how I would feed the people, and I clarified that it's not about physically feeding them but about feeding them spiritually.

Whispers of the Holy Spirit

Palm Sunday, 28-3-2021- I attended the Divine Retreat Centre in Somersby, where, as a volunteer, I assisted retreatants waiting to receive the Sacrament of Reconciliation.

A lady was waiting to go in next, and she asked me why we no longer pray in tongues as we are Charismatics. During Adoration, many people often pray using the gift of tongues, but it has been a long time since we were encouraged to pray in Tongues.

My reply to her was, "If you are praying and you feel the power of the Holy Spirit dwelling within you, and you desire to pray in tongues, then you must pray in tongues. Do not worry about the person next to you or around you." I told her that when I'm driving, I'm always praying. Sometimes, the power of the Holy Spirit moves within me, and I begin to pray in tongues. Spending a lot of timeg on the road gives me plenty of opportunity to pray and speak to God. Talking to God from my heart while driving is a comforting and reassuring experience. I often feel His presence around me while driving. I have my praise and worship hymns playing and my personal time of praise and worship with God.

Sometimes, I feel so moved by the Holy Spirit that it brings tears to my eyes while driving. It's no surprise to me that God chose to tell me to write a book, A Woman of Faith, while I was behind the wheel. God is everywhere; you do not find Him only in the church. He is always with us. He tells us to: "Be strong and of good courage, do not fear or be in dread of them: for it is the Lord your God who goes with you; he will not fail you or forsake you." (Deuteronomy 31:6).

I went through a stage when I was afraid to drive further than 30 km. One day, I had no option but to drive that far, so I prayed fervently, asking God to be with me, to go before me as I drove, and to take away my fear of driving. I surrendered everything to the Lord. He answered my prayers, and I drove there and back without fear. I knew the Lord heard my prayers and took away all anxiety and fear from me. I felt at peace, and a calm presence surrounded me. After that day, I drove all over, confident that God was with me and protecting me while I was driving. Fear is not of God. I have known so many people who fear driving beyond their surrounding areas.

I say to you, trust in God and surrender your fears to Him. Don't let the evil one convince you; you cannot venture beyond your neighbourhood. Allow God to be in control. Have faith and believe that Prayer is powerful.

During this time, adoration took place, and we could hear every word Father was saying from where we were waiting. Within two minutes of saying this, Fr. Roni told us to keep praying and to use the gift of tongues. Although I was not directly in front of the Blessed Sacrament, like everyone else, my faith was strong enough to believe that God was with me during this time of Adoration, feeling His ever-loving presence surround me. I looked at the lady and told her that The Holy Spirit had heard her desire to pray in tongues; even though we were not physically in front of the Blessed Sacrament, we were praying in our hearts as if we were, since we could hear the prayers being recited.

"And they were all filled with the Holy Spirit and began to speak in other tongues as the Spirit gave them utterance." (Acts 2: 45 – 46).

"And the believers from among the circumcised who came with Peter were amazed because the gift of the Holy Spirit had been poured out even on the Gentiles. For they heard them speaking in tongues and extolling God." (Acts 10: 45-46).

Spiritual gifts can be found in 1 Corinthians 12: 1-11

When God Reveals the Truth

I work in Aged Care, and I enjoy helping the elderly. I learn a lot from them because they are wise, and full of experience. I treat them as I would treat my parents and grandparents if they were still alive today. In my adult life, I never got the chance to know or care for my grandparents, as they passed this life when I was still very young. My mom died when I was just two months old, and I was in Australia when my dad passed away.

On a few occasions, I visited a client who had cancer, and after about three months, she was no longer on my roster. I always wondered what had happened to her. One day, I had some free time and suddenly felt inspired to sit in front of the Blessed Sacrament on my way home. I was less than five minutes away from a church when I felt this inspiration.

I entered the church, expecting to find the Blessed Sacrament exposed on the altar. Since it wasn't there, I decided to leave. As I was walking out, I heard a whisper saying, "Look," so I looked up. In front of me was a glass cabinet against the wall, and inside it was a memorial booklet for the client. I was curious to find out what had happened to her. I recognised the photo because it was the same one she had displayed in her lounge.

I was so upset I burst into tears, as if in shock. I wasn't prepared for what I had seen. That was the only booklet in the glass cabinet, and there was nothing else. I was the only person there. Had I not followed the prompting of the Holy Spirit, I wouldn't have discovered what had happened to her, nor would I have seen the booklet, if not for the whisper I heard to "look", as I had already passed the glass cabinet upon entering the church.

That day, the Lord planted a desire in my heart to visit a particular church, so I could see the Memorial booklet in the cabinet and find closure. I don't belong to that parish, so I don't attend Mass there. He knew I longed to discover what had happened to her. I am always amazed when God understands what you are going through and acts swiftly to answer and clarify the truth you seek. He is the Alpha and the Omega, the only true God.

On Sunday, 29th September 2024, during a talk at the Retreat Centre, the Spirit of God enlightened me about the day I had a vision in front of the Blessed Sacrament. I had finished work a little early, so I went to the parish where I usually visit the Blessed Sacrament.

One day, while praying, my eyes were fixed on the Monstrance, which held the Eucharistic Lord. I saw a vision of an eye, and the eyeball spun around. The area around it was brightly lit. It lasted for a few seconds. I was in awe and felt that the Lord was watching me as I knelt before Him and that He heard my prayers. My prayers always included inspiration for this book, which I was still writing, and I kept asking whether it was His will for the book to be published.

"The eyes of the Lord are toward the righteous, and his ears toward their cry." (Psalm 34:15).

Chapter 18

The 15-Year Prayer That Changed Everything

My eldest daughter moved out of our home and moved in with her girlfriends, sharing a house that belonged to the parents of one of her friends.

After about two years, she introduced her boyfriend to us. They had been seeing each other for a while. I soon realised that he lacked faith and didn't believe in God. He sensed that something is out there but refused to accept it. I had only just met him and wasn't about to question why he didn't believe. I didn't know how long the relationship would last. We made him feel welcome, as this is what Christ expects of us.

After a few years, they conceived a child, and we were blessed with a grandson. This was my first grandchild, whom I loved deeply and still do. As I was unemployed at the time, I could play a highly active role in his life when my daughter returned to work.

I used to take him to Mass every Wednesday at a neighbouring parish. I introduced him to the Mass and taught him how to pray. Many years later, when he was in primary school, he told me that his Scripture teacher said he knew everything about Jesus and the Catholic faith. She asked how he knew all the answers in Scripture classes, and he told her that his gran teaches him. I had the privilege of meeting her one day at a sports event, and she said to me, "So, you are the grandmother who is teaching your grandson." I felt blessed that day, knowing the foundation was laid.

My daughter and her partner decided to do the right thing and get married, so they moved in with us to save some money. Although they were married in the Catholic Church, he still didn't quite believe. I faced a challenge. I kept talking about God the Father and Jesus, our Lord and Saviour. He would try to challenge me every time I spoke about Jesus.

During prayer nights, I always invited him to join us but never pressured him. He would sit outside while we held family prayers. He was adamant that he wouldn't join us for prayers, and my daughter would tell me not to force him.

I prayed for his conversion after I got to know him. I never once gave up. Sometimes, I wondered whether he would ever change. God sees and hears everything that we say and do. We often look for a quick fix. When we pray, we seek instant answers, but God knows when the time is right, which can mean waiting years for

His response. We are tested to see how long we will persevere in prayer. Do we give up after a few weeks or months? Do we allow Satan to take hold and tell us that God will never answer our prayers? Some prayers are answered instantly, while others take years to unfold.

St Monica prayed for St Augustine for 17 years before his conversion to Christianity. Her persistent prayers paid off, and St Augustine eventually changed his life completely. He became a priest and later a Bishop. He is well known for his writings, especially his book "Confessions of St. Augustine." I have included a few of his quotes in this book. I prayed for 15 years for my son-in-law's conversion to the Catholic Faith. I never gave up; I knew God would answer when the time was right.

When I first started attending the Retreat Centre monthly, I wanted my daughters to participate with their husbands, so for my birthday, I asked that they attend the Last Sunday Retreat with my husband and me during that month. They agreed. I felt happy and hoped that the Lord would touch their hearts and that they would start attending church regularly.

Meanwhile, I continued praying for my son-in-law's conversion. I later found out that he felt genuinely moved by the Holy Spirit during the retreat he attended, which happened to be the month of my birthday. I knew that God had planted the seed, and now I had to pray for that seed to grow.

I will always be grateful that my grandson went to a Catholic School and that his father supported his religious beliefs. My son-in-law was also educated at a Catholic School, but for some reason, he still did not believe in God.

In 2022, my son-in-law surprised me by telling me he wanted to become a Catholic. I asked him if he was certain and if that was what he genuinely wanted, and he replied 'Yes'.

He wanted to share the same religious beliefs as my daughter and grandson. I was shocked because I wasn't prepared for what I had just heard. I felt pleased to hear to those words, but also uncertain if he would see this journey of conversion through to the end. After speaking to him, I went and prayed, thanking Jesus for planting the seed and for hearing and answering my prayers after fifteen years of praying. When I asked my daughter if this was what her husband wanted, she also said she was surprised. As joint Coordinator for RCIA in our parish, I sat down with him and explained the Rite of Christian Initiation of Adults (RCIA) and what is expected of him. He seemed adamant that this was what he wanted.

Our parish was planning to organise a Marian Fiesta in October 2022. Each year, a different community has the opportunity to hosts this event. Our parish priest, Fr. Michael Belonio, asked me if the South African and Mauritian groups could host the Marian Fiesta, as the originally selected group was unable to do so that year. I was caught off guard and unprepared for this, as I understood the amount of work and stress involved in organising the event, which we had previously hosted around six years earlier. It is also a major fundraising event, the biggest on our parish calendar. Unfortunately, we hadn't held the Marian Fiesta for two years due to COVID-19. Our parish was in serious need of financial support after the pandemic's impact.

I asked my daughter and son-in-law if they could help with our committee. Surprisingly, they both agreed. Joe and I decided to go ahead with Fr. Michael's request, as I couldn't bring myself to say no to a priest, since they represent Christ. We managed to find a few people; some had been on the committee the first time we hosted the Fiesta. This was to be the first time my son-in-law got involved in anything related to the church. I began to see a change come over him. He became incredibly involved and very dedicated in the planning of the Marian Fiesta.

The Fiesta was a remarkable success, and a substantial amount of money was raised to support the daily operations of our parish. This was the first test, and my son-in-law passed with flying colours.

He joined the RCIA Journey, and there was a time when I thought he would give up and walk away. He needed to find a Sponsor and a Godparent or Godparents. He knew the criteria for choosing a Sponsor and Godparent. The friend he had asked wasn't a practising Catholic, but he still wanted him to be his Godparent. He said he didn't want to ask me because I already had plenty to do, and I was his mother-in-law.

I was praying that he found the right person. My daughter was his Sponsor, so I suggested she not take on the role of Godparent as well. A few weeks before he had to submit the name of his Godparent, he found out that his friend would be away at Easter; therefore, he would not be able to be his Godparent. He was devastated, and this is when he wanted to give up and walk away.

I advised him to find a quiet spot, read his Bible, pray, and ask God to help him choose the right person to be his Godparent. I told him, "That while you are praying, the name that comes to your mind will be the person God is telling you to choose". Not long after, I received a call from him, and he told me that my name had come to him during prayer, and he asked if I could be his Godparent. He said he didn't want to ask me, as I was already doing so much. I then explained to him that whether he was there or not,

I would still have to go every week. I was not going out of my way in any way.

He finally agreed. I then told him that I was not happy with his first choice for his godparent, only because he would not be able to provide the spiritual guidance, he would need during his journey of conversion. There is so much to learn about the faith. God guided you to make the right decision. He felt relieved when I said yes. He was fully baptised into the Catholic faith at the Easter Vigil Mass 2022.

Prayer is powerful, as God already knows what we will ask him before we can ask." Whatever you ask in my name, I will do it, that the Father may be glorified in the Son. If you ask anything in my name, I will do it." (John 14:13-14).

It took 15 years of prayers, but I never gave up. God works in His own time. Only He knows when the moment is right. We must face many challenges along our journey, and He will determine how strong our faith is and how resilient we are. Do we believe God will answer when He knows the perfect time has come? Sometimes, when we think, God hasn't responded to our prayers, we feel He has abandoned us, but that isn't true. If we don't receive what we pray for, it might be that the timing isn't right, or perhaps it's not meant for us to have what we asked for. That's also an answer to our prayer. We are human and believe we know what suits us, but only God knows when the perfect time is right. Do not be disheartened if God takes a while to answer your prayers. If it is meant for you, He will answer in his own time.

In today's society, we have become too accustomed to instant gratification. We have instant messaging services like Instagram, Twitter (now called X), Messenger, emails, and Facebook. In the past, we had to walk or drive to the Post Office or use a postal van if we needed to send a letter. Mail took a few weeks, if you were lucky enough to get a reply, but we accepted it because there was no other choice. Be patient. Before you ask Him, God knows what you need, so trust Him.

"Do not be like them, for your Father knows what you need before you ask him." (Matthew 6:8).

Chapter 19

Learning to Abide in Love

Our Parish has the Exposition of the Blessed Sacrament on the first Friday of each month. The Spirituality Commission Group, which consist of five members, including myself, organises this in our parish. It is a time set aside to spend in the presence of Our Lord.

On the first Friday, the 3rd of June 2022, I decided to pray and ask God to reveal to me what He wanted me to write in the book A Woman of Faith. I took a small notepad with me, and I had a pen in my bag that had been there for a few days. After praying for a while, I decided to take out the notepad and pen to start writing. When

I reached into my bag to retrieve the pen, it was broken having come apart. I knew the pen was originally intact, so I was extremely disappointed because I couldn't write anything that the Spirit of The Lord might reveal.

I realised that it was not pleasing to the Lord. Our Lord wanted me to sit quietly and feel His omniscient presence around me, speaking to Him from the depths of my heart and listening to Him. To be still and know He is God. I felt so guilty and sad that I visited Him in the Blessed Sacrament with those intentions. Our plans and God's plans are vastly different. Only He knows His plans for us. We need to strengthen our relationship with Him and continually obey His calling. We need to allow Him to be in control and trust that He will care for us when we go to Him for help.

As I sat there praying, the Spirit of The Lord gave me this word: ABIDE. I was startled when I heard the phrase, as I realised that Jesus knew my intentions before I left home. The Gospel of John speaks of abide- v7 "If you abide in me, and my words abide in you, ask whatever you will, and it shall be done for you. v 9 As the Father has loved me, so have I loved you; abide in my love." (John, 15:1-11).

I felt that Jesus was telling me to abide in His love, to be filled with the Word of God, simply to be there, sitting in His presence, listening to Him, believing in Him, and feeling His love surround me. I want to get to know Him intimately and allow Him to change my heart so that I may love as He loves us and remain in Him to be fruitful. He wanted me to trust Him and have a close relationship with Him so that I could believe that whatever I asked in His name, he would give it to me.

From that day forward, I no longer take a notepad when I sit before the Blessed Sacrament. I begin with prayer, make my petitions, and then sit in silence, ready to hear God's voice speaking to me in the depths of my heart.

The Silent Power of Prayer

When you pray, do so privately without seeking public attention. Remember, prayer is not a monologue but a dialogue. You speak to God, then pause to listen for His response. "But when you pray, go into your room, and shut the door and pray to your Father who is in secret; and your Father who sees in secret will reward you." (Matthew 6: 6).

Most of the time, our prayers start with asking God to heal us, help us, and provide a job if we are unemployed. We also pray for our families and ask for changes in our family situation, especially for our children, as they might be heading down a destructive path. We ask Jesus to help them return to the straight and narrow road. Most people pray for these things; there is nothing wrong with this form of prayer.

Our first prayer should always be to praise God, just as David always did. Thank Him for everything He has done and given us to enable us to live on this earth, as He created the Heavens and the earth. We praise His Holy name, which is above all other names.

We then thank Him for all the blessings we've received throughout the day. Thank Him for our families, our jobs, the roof over our heads, and for protecting us and returning us safely back to our loved ones after a day at work. Thank Him for the daily meals, the car you drive, the air you breathe, and all His beautiful creations. There is so much to thank God for. Be grateful for everything He has done and given us. Do not take anything for granted.

Following our expressions of gratitude, we turn to repentance. Here, we humbly ask God to forgive us for any intentional or unintentional wrongdoings and harm we may have caused others. It's a time to reflect on our actions and seek reconciliation with God.

We then proceed to make our prayer request. Here, we pray to God that if you need prayers in any area of your life, such as for a job, financial struggles, healing if you are unwell, or the well-being of your family,

You now pray for others. Here, we offer prayers for all those who have asked us to pray for them. Submit their intention to God. Generally, pray for people facing ill health or financial hardship. Pray for the homeless, poor, lonely, and destitute. Pray for peace in the world and war-torn countries.

After expressing all our intentions, we listen to God's voice within our hearts. Sitting in silence is always a challenge, as our minds quickly drift to the events of the day, thinking about work and the children. We often become distracted by our surroundings. We forget that we should be listening to God, who speaks to us in the silence of our hearts.

"Be still and know that I am God. I am exalted among the nations; I am exalted in the earth." (Psalm 46:10).

Prayer is a dialogue with God. When we speak to God, it is a conversation between you and Him. He invites us to open up to Him about our difficulties and sorrows and acknowledge Him for the good he has done in our lives. Just speak to him as though you were talking to a friend. He loves you and cares for you. Find a quiet place to pray, away from noise and distractions.

When Jesus prayed to His Heavenly Father, He always went alone to quiet places to be one with God. Before He started His ministry, He was Baptised by John the Baptist. "Now when all the people were baptized and when Jesus also had been baptized and was praying, the heaven was opened, and the Holy Spirit descended upon him in bodily form, as a dove, and a voice came from heaven, "You are my beloved Son; with you I am well pleased."" (Luke 3:21- 22).

After Jesus was baptised, He went into the desert for forty days to pray and fast. The devil tried to tempt him many times when he was most vulnerable, as He was weak, tired, and hungry. Jesus never gave in to Satan's temptations. Satan knows Scripture and tries to use it to tempt Jesus, and he will use it to tempt us as well.

Jesus went out to the hills and prayed all night before He chose the Twelve Apostles and also the night before He was to die, in the Garden of Gethsemane, where He was filled with great sorrow and distress and prayed to His Father in such anguish that his sweat was like drops of blood falling to the ground, asking His Father to take the cup of suffering away from Him.

Jesus was both human and Divine. God sent His angels to comfort Him in his times of distress. He always wanted to be alone in isolated places where He could speak to his Father privately.

God, always attentive, answers our prayers and sends human angels to aid us. His responses may not always align with our requests, but they are always what He knows is best for us. Pray to God, then meditate and listen for His guidance. His voice is heard in the silence, guiding us in our journey.

Jesus taught us how to pray by giving us this beautiful prayer, the Our Father, in which we come to know, love, and understand the Heavenly Father. It is the prayer that we recite during the Eucharistic prayers.

Our Father—Jesus invites us to share His Father, calling Him Our Father. This inclusion makes us part of God's family, surpassing race, colour, and creed, uniting us all as His children.

Who art in Heaven - God sits on the throne in Heaven, where we hope to meet Him one day when we return to our Heavenly home, our final destiny.

Hallowed be thy name - We honour the Father and give reverence to his Holy name by saying Hallowed be thy name and acknowledging His Holiness. We should never commit blasphemy against God's Holy name, as His name is above all other names.

Thy Kingdom come -This phrase reminds us that God is not just our Father, but also a King. His kingdom is our ultimate destination. As a loving Father, He sacrificed His only Son for us, preparing the way for our repentance and return to Him.

Thy will be done on earth as it is in Heaven- God expects us to live a holy life and to be obedient to the Ten Commandments given to Moses from God.

Give us this day our daily bread — The bread is consecrated during the Mass, becoming the real living bread that came down from Heaven. The Eucharist nourishes our souls and helps us live a spiritual life pleasing to God. When the Israelites wandered in the desert for 40 years, they complained of hunger. God heard their grumblings. "Then the Lord said to Moses," Behold, I will rain bread from heaven for you; and the people shall go out and gather a day's portion every day, that I may test them, whether they will walk in my law or not. On the sixth day, when they prepare what they bring in, it will be twice as much as they gather daily.'" (Exodus 16 4-5).

And Forgive us our Trespasses as we forgive those who Trespass against us – We ask the Father for forgiveness for our sins, just as we should forgive those who have offended us. This act of forgiveness is crucial in our relationship with God and others. God, being merciful and full of love, knows our weakness. If we are remorseful and seek forgiveness with a sincere and contrite heart, He will forgive us for our wrongdoings. We cannot ask God for His forgiveness if we cannot forgive our brothers and sisters in Christ. When you forgive, you set yourself free. Jesus tells us how many times we should forgive one another." I do not say to you seven times, but seventy times seven." (Mathew 18:22)

And lead us not into temptation—We pray and ask God to give us the strength to rebuke Satan in our moments of weakness. We seek His guidance to help us be firm in our faith and beliefs and to provide us with the grace to return to Him with a clean and contrite heart. This prayer emphasises the importance of God's guidance in our spiritual journey, especially in resisting temptation.

Deliver us from evil – God has granted us free will, but often, we choose paths that displease Him. When we sin, we distance ourselves from God, leaving us vulnerable to Satan's allure. We easily fall into the trap of repeating habitual sins, sometimes forgetting that they offend God. The actual danger of sin lies in finding pleasure in the pain we cause others. Therefore, we must constantly pray, seeking deliverance from the evil one. Remember, God is our protector, ready to deliver us from all evil.

Chapter 20

The Message Behind Parousia

On Wednesday night, 7th February 2024, I reviewed some of the pages I had printed for this book. I then pulled out the page with the writings regarding the time I heard the Spirit of the Lord say Parousia. While reading it, my phone alerted me to an incoming message, so I glanced at it and realised the message was from Fr. Roni.

I continued reading, and when I had finished, I read the message, which said the priest who was to conduct the retreat had to cancel as he had been asked to say Mass in a remote area over the weekend. Charbel Raish from Parousia will be conducting the retreat. When

I saw the name Parousia, I was surprised, as I was reading about Parousia at that exact moment. I said, 'Lord, what are you trying to tell me?'

I now have the opportunity to meet the owner of Parousia Media. I believe God plans everything. Never doubt the work of God, as He is the Almighty One. The God of all creation. He gave us a beautiful retreat; it was spiritually inspiring, and I discovered a great deal, which helped me understand some scripture readings in a new light.

On the last day of the retreat, I had an opportunity to speak with him and explain how I received the word Parousia. I told him I had called his business, Parousia Media, on the Monday after receiving the word Parousia on Sunday morning. I was trying to understand what the Divine message regarding Parousia entailed. Parousia means the second coming. What is Jesus trying to warn us about?

When I arrived home that evening after the retreat, I prayed to God, asking Him for help and guidance for this book. I prayed first and allowed the Spirit of the Lord to guide me in choosing one of the readings from the list that Fr. Antony had given me the previous week. I did not memorise any of the readings, so I was not familiar with what each verse contained. The reading I was guided to was – "I will not leave you desolate; I will come to you." (John 14:18).

This gave me hope, and I believe that God will help and be with me throughout the writing of this book. I could not have done this alone, as I never thought I would one day write a Spiritual book.

Chapter 21

Why Praying for Priests is Vital for the Church

Our priests are Shepherds whom God calls to care for His flock. In Exodus 28-29, Aaron and his brothers were the first called by God to be ordained as priests. We do not own them or have any hold over them; they are called to the Priesthood by God.

A few years ago, I felt a strong calling to pray for priests. I genuinely believe this is what God called me to do, so I started praying for priests and more vocations to the priesthood and Religious

Life. I was fortunate to join a Global Prayer Group, which later established an auxiliary group for those who desired to pray for priests and the religious life. There is a shortage of priests worldwide, so we need to pray for our priests and for more vocations to the priesthood.

Without priests, there is no Mass. Therefore, we cannot be nourished by the Holy Eucharist, the Source and Summit of our Christian Life. (2nd Vatican Council). This is the Bread of Life that has come down from heaven, the Body of Christ. Only ordained clergy can celebrate the Holy Mass. The Mass is the highest form of Worship. During the prayers of consecration of the bread and wine, it is transformed into the body and blood of Christ (Transubstantiation). Only through Faith do we believe we consume the Body and Blood of Christ when we receive Holy Communion.

We can only receive the Sacrament of Reconciliation with a priest, as only an Ordained Priest is authorised to administer it. We should go to the Sacrament of Reconciliation as often as possible since this keeps us close to God. When we sin, we separate ourselves from God.

Some people disrespect their priests, verbally abuse them, or want to control and tell them how to run their parishes or religious life. When you disrespect a priest, you are not only disrespecting them but also Christ. All priests represent Christ; therefore, we should show them respect.

Jesus has asked us to pray for the Catholic Church. We all represent the church, which is currently under attack in many ways. Many believe it is unnecessary to attend church, but now, more than ever, we must go to Mass. We need to find strength to face the many daily challenges in our lives. By attending Mass and receiving the Body of Christ, we can strengthen ourselves through regularly consuming Holy Communion. Those who are sick or bedridden are exempted from attending Mass. Usually, a Priest, Deacon, or Minister of the sick will visit them. We should make it our duty to attend Mass at least once a week.

"For the lips of a priest should guard knowledge, and men should seek instruction from his mouth for he is the messenger of the Lord of host." (Malachi 2:7).

Do not slander a priest's name. If they have hurt you, entrust them to God, pray for them, or seek guidance from someone on how to approach the situation. Let us not be judgmental, as we are not perfect. Do not listen to the voice of Satan, for he is working extremely hard to destroy the Church. Priests are human, just like us, and can make mistakes as we do. They also receive the Sacrament of Reconciliation. They have left their families and given up everything to follow God's calling to the Priesthood. They experience emotions just like everyone else. Every four to five years, most priests are transferred to a different parish, usually in another Diocese, meaning they must start their vocation as parish priest or assistant parish priest, getting to know everyone and learning how the parish usually operates. This takes time, so be patient with them, get to know them, and make them feel welcome. When sick and lonely, they sometimes have no one to turn to for help. Some live alone and can become very lonely. Most reside in foreign countries and have no family nearby to support them. Please respect, pray, and support your priests as they represent Christ. Now more than ever, priests need our prayers.

"But you are a chosen race, a royal priesthood, a holy nation, God's own people, that you may declare the wonderful deeds of him who called you out of darkness into his marvelous light." (1 Peter 2:9).

Chapter 22

The Dream That Urged Me to Pray for the World's Redemption

In the early hours of 11th March 2024. I had a very unsettling dream. I found myself at a place that looked like a retreat centre for religious gatherings. Many people were staying there for the weekend. It had a chapel on the grounds

On Sunday morning, everyone packed up and got ready to vacate the premises. Many people headed to the chapel to pray before going home.

I, too, was walking towards the chapel with a few others ahead of me, and as I was walked, I was told to pray for Redemption. There was a sense of urgency, as if prayers were desperately needed for the world's Redemption. In the dream, I kept repeating the word" Redemption," feeling a profound need to remember it. This urgency in prayer for redemption is a call to action, a commitment we must all make to bring light into the world.

I soon felt a powerful urgency to pray the Rosary, especially for the Redemption of the world. At that moment, it seemed vital to invoke the powerful intercession of Our Blessed Mother. for the salvation of souls and the conversion of sinners. Let us ask Our Blessed Mother to intercede for the Redemption of the entire world. Jesus came into the world to redeem us from the bondage of sin, as he paid the ultimate price on the cross.

"In him we have redemption through his blood, the forgiveness of our trespasses, according to the riches of his grace which he lavished upon us." (Ephesians 1:7-8).

As I was waking from sleep, I kept repeating the word redemption. Please pray for the conversion of sinners and for deliverance from the bondage of sin so that we may be reconciled with God.

Three Signs from the Book of Amos

On the 16 March 2024, I sat down to read the Bible, and as usual, I prayed first, asking God to speak to me through His word. I opened the Bible, and it fell open to Amos Chapter 1. I have never read the book of Amos, nor has it ever been opened to Amos on previous occasions. I started reading and realised it was all about God bringing punishment and transgressions on Israel's neighbours. After reading a few verses, I closed the bible, said a prayer, and when I opened it again, it opened to Amos. So, I closed it the second time, and when it opened again, it opened to Amos. This was now the third consecutive time. I had no choice but to read what God was trying to draw my attention to.

Amos was a herdsman and a dresser of sycamore trees. The Lord called him to prophesy to the people of Israel, even though he was not a prophet. As I read, I was surprised to read about Gaza. I had never come across this word in any of the Bible readings I have read, except on the map at the back of my Bible. From chapter 1:6-8 God speaks about not revoking the punishment upon Israel's neighbours, and in chapter 3, God speaks of Israel's transgressions and punishment. I found these readings very intriguing as there is currently conflict in the Middle East between Israel and Gaza. I believe God has brought the current crises in the Middle East to my attention.

Please pray for the war to end in the Middle East and between Russia and Ukraine so peace may engulf these countries. Amos's message is about Justice and how God demands Justice for all.

"But let justice roll down like waters. And righteousness like an ever-flowing stream." (Amos 5:24).

A Glimpse of the Golden City

A few years ago, I had a dream of the New Jerusalem. In the dream, I saw a city surrounded by high walls made of gold that was descending from the sky. It wasn't a massive city but a miniature version of the city of Jerusalem. It was decorated with precious stones, like diamonds, rubies, opals, sapphires, emeralds, and many others. Some colours included red, green, and clear crystal-like stones that sparkled. I was amazed at the beauty of the entire city, crafted from pure gold and precious stones. I was in awe and wondered about beauty that could only come from God. I woke up before the city could reach the ground.

I had read a little about the New City of Jerusalem in the Book of Revelation many years ago, long before I had the dream. I don't usually read the Book of Revelation. After the dream, I realised it is written in Revelation 21: 9-21, where John describes what he sees in a vision of the New Jerusalem. When I got out of bed in the morning, I was still amazed at the beauty I had seen in the dream. I didn't see anything else, no people were around, and I didn't feel the Spirit of the Lord speak to me. In the dream, I knew it was the New Jerusalem.

Could a New Car Be God's Answer to Serving Strangers with Love

In 2016, after many years of service, my car started having problems. As we regularly drove to the Central Coast and took other people with us twice a month, we had to consider buying a new car, mainly for safety reasons, as we were also carrying other passengers.

On the 29th of February 2016, I turned to the Lord seeking his advice on whether we should buy a new car or continue repairing the one we had, as well as for the safety of our passengers, who on most occasions, were people we hadn't met before. They would tell me that a friend had given them my mobile number so they could call and ask if we could give them a lift if we were heading to Somersby. After my prayer, I opened my Bible, which opened to Hebrews Chapter 13, "Sacrifices Well - Pleasing to the Lord. v1-2 reads, "Let brotherly love continue. Do not neglect to show hospitality to strangers, for thereby some have entertained angels unawares."

V20-21 "Now may the God of peace, (...) equip you with everything good that you may do his will, working in you that which is pleasing in his sight, through Jesus Christ; to whom be glory for ever and ever. Amen" (Hebrews 13:1-22).

When I read this chapter, I realised God had answered my prayer, and we were blessed to buy a new car. We have continued to offer lifts to anyone who needs one to Somersby Retreat Centre.

Finding God's Comfort in Distress

On 14 October 2015 while in a previous job, I experienced a moment of distress due to a particular situation at the time. On my way home from work that day, I wanted to sit in front of the Blessed Sacrament; I stopped at my parish only to find that the gates were locked. I went home, sat at my prayer table, and surrendered everything to God. After praying, I opened my Bible, and the reading my eyes fell upon was. (…) "they ought always to pray and not lose heart". (Luke 18: 1-8).

God sees everything and knows everything we are experiencing, and we are never alone. Whenever I desire to feel close to God, I sit quietly and pray, then open the Word of God, as God reveals all through his Word, the Holy Bible. It was only shortly after that I found another job. I have always tried to live a life that is pleasing to God. I sometimes fail, but I pray and ask God to help me get back on the straight and narrow road. I am never boastful and have a quiet nature. Whatever I do, I always strive to do everything for the Glory of God. He knows us and understands us better than we understand ourselves.

White Garment and Gathering Crowds: Awaiting the Unseen Miracle"

Two dreams have yet to come true. One dream I had was that my wardrobe was empty, except for a white garment hanging over the lower railing in my built-in wardrobe. It was long, folded over the railing, and nearly touched the ground. The white garment has a spiritual meaning, representing purity and righteousness. I saw a white garment on the altar at my first healing Mass.

The other dream I had was at the Retreat Centre. Many people were present that day, and the grounds were full to capacity, with the crowd extending towards the Centre's main entrance. After lunch, there was a Eucharistic Procession, which started from the Adoration Chapel near the Dining Hall. We were all waiting for the priest to reach the main Hall's entrance.

There have been many Eucharistic Processions when praying the Way of the Cross around the grounds. The difference in the dream is the direction of the procession with the Eucharist. The procession stops at the entrance to the Main Hall, and the priest and acolytes face the grounds, not entering the Main Hall. We are waiting for something to happen, which is why so many people are in attendance. I cannot guarantee this will materialise, but it would be wonderful if a miracle where to take place.

Chapter 23

A Call to Honor the Sacredness of God's Dwelling

W riting this causes me great sorrow, but I do so because Jesus tells me in the Book of Tobit, 'To write everything in a book that has happened to you.'

A few years ago, during Mass, I was sitting towards the front of the church when suddenly I felt the Spirit of the Lord speak to me. I was drawn to some children old enough to understand the Mass, who were eating and colouring in their books instead of being attentive to what was happening at the altar. Jesus loves children:

"(...) "Let the children come to me, and do not hinder them; for to such belongs the kingdom of God." (Luke 15:16). This behaviour can be tolerated by little toddlers who don't understand what is happening during the Mass. All children are welcomed at Mass, as they are the future generation, where they will eventually, as they grow older, begin to understand what is happening during the Mass.

There is a distinction between our home and the House of God. The church is God's dwelling; we visit it to honour the King of Kings and the Lord of Lords. When we enter the church, we should remember that we are truly in the presence of God and Our Lord Jesus Christ. We should genuflect facing the altar. We should be prayerful, spend time with God, and prepare ourselves before we participate in the Holy Mass.

Do we dress respectfully when we visit the sacred house of the Lord? Is our behaviour in the house of God pleasing to the Lord? There is a saying," Come as you are," and we often misinterpret this. It does not mean we should dress disrespectfully. We come as we are, broken, sinful, and weary, seeking God's mercy and forgiveness. God welcomes us into His sacred presence, regardless of the state of our hearts. It is a holy opportunity to reconcile with God Our Father; our behaviour should reflect this. The Bible tells us:

"I desire then that in every place that the men should pray, lifting holy hands without anger or quarreling; also, that women should adorn themselves modestly and sensibly in seemly apparel, not with braided hair or gold or pearls or costly attire but by good deeds, as befits women who profess religion. "(1 Timothy 2:8-10).

I was then inspired to observe someone checking their mobile phone during Mass. We should turn off our phones or put them on silent mode when we are attending Mass. I was then made aware that people are talking during the Mass, oblivious to what is taking place on the altar, especially during the prayers of consecration, where transubstantiation takes place, meaning when the bread and wine become the real presence of the body and blood of Christ, but there is no physical change in the appearance of the bread and wine. When we receive the Eucharist, we consume the body of Christ.

"The Eucharistic presence of Christ begins at the moment of the consecration and endures as long as the Eucharistic species subsist. Christ is present whole and entire in each of the species and whole and entire in each of their parts, in such a way that the breaking of the bread does not divide Christ." (CCC:1377).

When the Spirit of the Lord revealed all this to me, I felt sad as I realised how the Lord hurts when he sees us behaving this way. I love the Lord my God with all my heart and soul and always strive to obey his will. When I am weak and fall, I humbly ask God to give me the Grace to be strong and faithful to his calling.

Let us be mindful of our behaviour in the House of God. It is God's dwelling place; therefore, we should respect His home. In the Holy Land, you cannot enter any church sleeveless. We had to be dressed appropriately; if you were wearing sleeveless clothing, you were told to wear a shawl to cover up. No one will be turned away for not wearing the appropriate attire. Everybody is welcome in the House of God but be mindful of our behaviour. Let us honour Him in the way that he deserves.

I am only the messenger; I must obey God and deliver His message as He asks. This is an accurate account of what happened. The Lord is present in His dwelling place, and He sees everything that is happening.

Chapter 24

Called to Be a Witness

On 21st April 2024, the Spirit of the Lord reminded me of when Jesus asked me to be a Witness. During one of the weekend retreats I attended during my first year, my name, along with a few others, was called out, and Fr. Michael Payyapilly said that the Lord was calling us to be His witnesses.

I wasn't sure what the Lord was asking of me at the time, so I wasn't sure how to be a witness for Jesus. I always acknowledged Jesus and spoke about him to family and friends. I know Jesus asked his apostles to go out and be his witnesses before he ascended into Heaven. "But you shall receive power when the Holy Spirit has come upon you; and you shall be my witnesses in Jerusalem and in all Judea, and Samaria, and to the end of the earth." (Acts 1:8).

I later realised that I had to speak about Jesus to others, not only family and friends but to everyone in society. I shouldn't be afraid of rejection but go out and be a witness for Him so that others may come to know, love, and accept Him as Lord and Saviour. It's about bringing the non-believer to Christ. When you try to speak of Jesus, the weak will always try to brush you off and pass sarcastic remarks, some jokingly but in their hearts, actually meaning what they are saying.

Some people think you only speak of Jesus in the confines of the church on Sunday morning. When you love someone, you always want to talk about them and share that love with others. Only when life takes a turn do they suddenly want to know Jesus.

You rarely see people in public places when they are about to eat, signing themselves with the cross and giving thanks to God. I still say grace in public areas and have instilled this practice in my children and grandson.

"So everyone who acknowledges me before men, I also will acknowledge before my Father who is in heaven; but whoever denies me before men, I also will deny before my Father who is in heaven". (Matthew 10: 32-33).

Sometimes, you don't need words to convey a message to someone; it is through your actions, as actions speak louder than words. We will pay dearly for disrespecting God the Father and His Son, our Lord Jesus Christ. We all have to answer to God on the day of judgment.

The word Parousia has come up a few times, and as I have discovered its true meaning, which refers to the Second Coming, let us live our lives as if that day is close at hand.

I hope and pray that through this book, I am a witness to many and that I can help those who are lost find the way back to God the Father and his Son, our Lord Jesus Christ, and believe that with God, nothing is impossible.

The Father waits to welcome you back home, just like the Parable of the Prodigal Son, in the Bible, Luke 15:11-32

Interrupted Vision: What Was the Message Behind the Radiant Golden Tiara

On Sunday, the 21 April 2024, I attended the 9:30 am Mass at our parish. I usually attend this Mass, except when I am away on Retreat. One of my ministries at our parish is serving as a Welcomer, which I have mentioned in an earlier chapter. When I am rostered most Sundays, I usually sit in the foyer in case people need to know or ask us anything. I typically get an opportunity to sit inside the church at least once a month unless there are five Sundays in the month.

At the end of the Mass, as we stood during Father Dave's final prayer and blessing, I had a beautiful vision of a golden tiara. It wasn't a complete circle but rather a partial one, not quite a crown. The light shining from behind the tiara was intensely bright, with each peak radiating a glow. The tiara was made of sparkling gold, without any jewels embedded in it. The brilliance of the gold and the surrounding light was simply stunning.

Unfortunately, I do not understand the meaning of this vision or the message God was trying to convey. My description does not do it justice, as it is difficult to put into words how beautiful it was. Even though there were no precious stones surrounding it, the band around the head was detailed. Nobody was wearing the tiara. As the Mass finished, people started to leave, and a lady was waiting for me to exit so she could go. Had I not been disturbed, I might have seen the full vision. I am trying to figure out if there was anything more to see or if I had seen the complete vision.

Chapter 25

Seeing God's Presence in Every Living Creature

On Monday, 30th September 2024, while driving to work, I had a fantastic experience with a bird.

I was driving along when suddenly I heard a shrieking sound. I looked to my right, and there was a medium-sized white bird with its wings spread out, walking in the opposite direction I was driving, making a loud noise. I looked at the bird and realised it was protecting its young, walking behind. At that moment, I was in awe of the Creator and His creation. I was so overwhelmed that tears streamed down my cheeks, and I cried out to God, thanking Him for His beautiful creation and this overwhelming experience, as I see God in everything He has made. Even a bird knows how to protect its fledgling. The timing was so perfect. This bird was trying to attract my attention to let me know that her baby was nearby and that I must not harm it. God created the heavens and the earth. In Genesis, we learn how God created the world.

"And God said. 'Let the waters bring forth swarms of living creatures and let birds fly above the earth across the firmament of the heavens.' v21(...) and every winged bird according to its kind. v22 And God blessed them, saying, 'Be fruitful and multiply and fill the waters in the seas, and let birds multiply on the earth.'" (Genesis 1:20-22).

I am always amazed at how all living creatures, large and small, know precisely how to care for their young. "So God created man in his own image, in the image of God he created him; male and female he created them. (Genesis 1:27)

Let us Glorify God for his marvellous creation in humans, animals, and every living creature.

Chapter 26

A Journey of Prayer and Miracles for a Little Life

I had mixed emotions when my youngest daughter told us she was expecting her second child. I was excited and happy for them. I always encouraged her to have a two-year gap between the first and second child. I was surprised; although excited, I suddenly felt sadness envelop me. I could not understand why, and it truly bothered me.

I did not say anything to her, for I knew she would want to know why I felt that way. It bothered me throughout her pregnancy. Little did I know what lay ahead of us.

A couple of months into her pregnancy. It was discovered that the baby she was carrying had a hole in her heart. She knew she was carrying a girl. Later, it was found that the baby's ventricles were not developing at the same rate. This was devastating news for all of us, especially my daughter and son-in-law. They were given the choice to terminate the pregnancy. When she told me, I was horrified. Thanks be to God; they made the right decision and chose not to terminate the pregnancy.

I was so relieved when they informed me of their decision. I told her I would pray that her baby's ventricles would start growing at the same rate and that the hole in the heart would heal. They were referred to one of the best children's cardiologists. She was now under the care of a cardiologist, and she needed to be transferred to Westmead Hospital, where she would give birth. Immediately after, her baby would be transferred to the Children's Hospital and placed in the Intensive Care Unit.

Miraculously, the ventricles grew to the same size after a few months, meaning she would not need surgery every 15 years. The hole in the heart was a blessing in disguise, allowing blood to flow to the right parts of the body.

My constant prayer was that the ventricles would grow to the same height. God heard our prayers and answered them. Often, when I had a little time during the day, I would visit the church where the Blessed Sacrament is exposed 24 hours a day. I always felt inspired to pray before the Blessed Sacrament, especially for the baby's healing. I would plead with God with tearful eyes, praying for the complete healing of this little baby growing in the womb. I believe wholeheartedly in the power of prayer.

I believed and had hope in the following words, "For with God nothing will be impossible." (Luke 1:37). "Therefore I tell you, whatever you ask in prayer, believe that you receive it, and you will." (Mark 11:24).

I prayed these verses daily. They gave me hope, as I had found solace in these words. I believed that God would answer our prayers, but each day brought worry. Every visit they had to the hospital, I felt anxious, praying that everything was going well with the baby. I always felt a wave of relief when they came back and said that the baby was doing well.

Under the circumstances, hearing those words was all I could hope for. It was heartbreaking for my daughter and son-in-law at every visit as they were told of the procedure and precisely what would happen after the delivery of their baby girl.

As the weeks went by, little miracles began to happen. I told my daughter that the first miracle was that the ventricles started growing at the same rate, and more miracles were yet to come. The surgeon recommended for the operation also had a child born in the same situation. God was great, and I could see His hand guiding every moment as they occurred. Although the condition was quite sad and hard to accept, I believed God had a plan in place, and I was confident everything would eventually turn out fine. I had to draw on every bit of Faith and not let doubt cloud my mind. I had to stay strong for my daughter.

As the time drew closer, the anxiety increased, and I had to keep reminding myself of the two bible verses that I placed all my faith and hope on. It was suggested to my daughter that it would be better for her to be induced one week before her due date to make sure that the team would all be available and ready for the delivery of the baby.

The cardiologist was concerned about the distance they would have to travel to get to the hospital if she unexpectedly went into labour during the middle of the night. They were advised that they could stay at the hospital as long as the baby was still recovering.

The day had now arrived for her to give birth, and it felt like the whole world had come to a stop while waiting for the news of the delivery. I was not able to be there as I had my granddaughter staying with us when she went into hospital. My eldest daughter and son-in-law were with her in the delivery room. The delivery went well, and the baby was taken away after about 10 minutes straight to the Children's Hospital and placed in the Newborn Intensive Care Unit.

My daughter sent us a photo of her baby, and my heart broke to see her, tiny body with tubes attached to help her breathe. She was also collecting fluid in the lungs, which made breathing difficult. She couldn't breastfeed for long because of her breathing troubles. So, a decision was made to feed her through a tube. The heart operation was scheduled for 7-10 days after birth.

The day finally arrived for the operation, and we were all anxious. The surgeon told my daughter and son-in-law it would be best for them to leave the hospital and not hang around. They would contact them as soon as the operation was complete.

I reached out to a few priests, including our parish priest, and asked them to please pray for our granddaughter as she undergoes open heart surgery. She was not even two weeks old when the operation took place. Unbeknownst to me, all the priests I contacted were about to celebrate Mass, and each one said they would offer the Mass for her. The Masses were celebrated in different time zones around the world. God's timing was perfect, and I knew then that she would be okay and that the surgery would be successful. The Mass is the highest form of Worship. This was a Blessing, and only God could have orchestrated such perfect timing.

I reached out to all the prayer groups I belong to and my friends, asking them to pray for my grandchild. Some are worldwide. Knowing that so many people across the globe were praying for our granddaughter brought me great comfort. I find solace and trust in the words of Jesus: "Therefore I tell you, whatever you ask in prayer, believe that you receive it, and you will." (Mark 11:24).

The day before the operation, I sat in front of the Blessed Sacrament, praying for a small miracle and for everything to go smoothly. On the day of the operation, I still felt a strong urge to sit before the Blessed Sacrament. It was the only place I wanted to be, as I felt close to Jesus, praying for the success of the operation. My daughter and her husband were struggling badly. They couldn't eat; were exhausted and emotionally upset.

The operation was scheduled to last five hours, and not long after the five hours were up, they were called to say they could return to the hospital. We waited in anticipation to find out the result of the operation. It was a relief to hear that everything went well, but the next twenty-four hours were critical. After her operation, she was moved to the Paediatric Intensive Care unit.

Her chest was left open to reduce swelling. She was heavily sedated, but the monitors kept beeping as her blood pressure dropped, and her heart rate remained high. The alarm sounded, and within a few minutes, the room was filled with the surgeon, doctors and nurses. She was given medication to stabilise her.

My daughter and son-in-law were told to prepare for the worst. She might have to be put on Life Support. The situation wasn't good, and they were both distressed and worried. This is the last thing you want to hear in this situation. She asked me to pray, which I did, and I also sent the message to the prayer groups to pray for my granddaughter. Prayer was all we could rely on during that time.

Praise God she stabilised after receiving the medication. God heard our prayers. Every day was a worry as her blood pressure kept dropping and her heart rate was dropping too low or going up too high. She was still accumulating fluid in her lungs. She had a pacemaker implanted at the time of surgery, which was to help her heart form its rhythm.

The first few days after the operation were the hardest, but gradually, she began to recover and stabilise. The machines continued to sound alarms while she was being monitored, and the room was once again filled with the medical team. When I visited her, it broke my heart to see all those tubes connected to her. Her body was too tiny to endure such major heart surgery. She tried to open her eyes when I spoke to her, so I knew she could hear my voice. But she was on so much medication that she was drowsy. I prayed for her and made the sign of the cross on her forehead.

I was beginning to worry about my daughter and son-in-law because they weren't getting enough sleep and weren't eating properly. They showed signs of exhaustion. The nurses advised them to rest, but they wanted to stay with their baby girl. It was a very distressing time for them. They were also concerned about their firstborn, who was staying with us while they were at the hospital.

I was pleasantly surprised that my granddaughter adapted so well while living with us. Having her stay with us brought us joy and pleasure, alleviating one concern for my daughter and son-in-law. Between both sets of grandparents, we cared after the 2-year-old toddler.

Every day, the baby was making remarkable progress. All her vital signs were improving, which was a relief. They closed up her chest four days after her operation, and everything went smoothly with the procedure. After the operation, she was moved to another ward indicating, she was coping well and getting ready to leave the hospital.

Every second day, they began removing her tubes and gradually tapering off her medication. The next step was to reintroduce breastfeeding to observe how she managed and whether she would become short of breath. She handled it quite well; it had been a few days since her last feed.

She was now approaching the day she would be discharged. All the tubes had been removed, she was coping well, and the doctors and specialists were all pleased with her progress. This was fantastic news for the family, especially my daughter and son-in-law. Three days later, after all the tubes were taken out and she was feeding well, she received the all-clear to go home.

This was the best news that we could have received. We call her our miracle baby. Seven days later, the stitches were removed and that went smoothly. The wound has healed well.

On Sunday, 24th November 2024, I had a lovely surprise at our parish. I sat at the back of the church when I looked up and saw my daughter walking in, pushing the pram. They don't live in our area, so I was surprised to see her. They were running late for their Mass because just as they were leaving for church, the toddler had spoiled her dress and needed to be changed That was when they decided to come to our parish.

I then saw my son-in-law and granddaughter walk in. I told my daughter that God works in mysterious ways. I was very happy to see them. It was quite fitting for them to be at that particular Mass, because our parish holds a blessing for all married couples married within that month every fourth Sunday followed by morning tea. My son-in-law's parents were married in November, so they went to the altar to have their marriage blessed. The group I belong to was responsible for organising the morning tea alongside another group my son-in-law's parents are part of. It was also a blessing that they attended our parish as a few members of the prayer groups who were praying for our grandchild, were there, which gave me the chance to introduce my daughter to them.

After Mass, I introduced my granddaughter to our parish priest, Fr Percival, and our assistant parish priests, who had been praying for her and offering multiple Masses since the day of her operation. I will always be immensely grateful to our parish priest for their prayers and support during the family's challenging time.

When I arrived for Mass that morning, he asked me how she was doing. He was surprised and happy to meet our granddaughter finally. I asked him and our assistant parish priest to bless her. God sure works in mysterious ways. I told my daughter that they were meant to be at our parish, as our whole parish was praying for her daughter.

I praise and thank God for this beautiful miracle, for nothing is impossible with God.

CONCLUSION

As I approach the conclusion of my writing, I have found that finishing this book has been a true joy and a blessing. I trusted and believed that God would help me to author this book, and without the Grace of God, I don't think I would have managed to complete it on my own. It has been an awe-inspiring experience for me, as I felt the presence of the Holy Spirit around me whenever I sat down to write. It required a great deal of Faith to complete this book. All praise and thanks be to God.

During the week from the end of April to the first week of May 2024, I noticed that after finishing the writing for this book, it felt as though some of its content had been read out to me through the priest in their sermons and watching talks given by priest on the YouTube channel.

April Last Sunday Retreat- Fr Rony spoke about the five stones of Mother Mary,

Prayer

Fasting

The Mass

The Bible

Confession

I have mentioned five of the stones in my writings. I talk about prayer and its importance, including listening to God, and meditating on the Word of God.

I also discussed the importance of fasting and our Blessed Mother's request to fast on Wednesdays and Fridays.

I emphasise the importance of priests' role in celebrating the Mass and the significance of attending Mass. Only ordained priests can administer the Sacrament of Reconciliation, and it is vital to visit this Sacrament regularly, as sin separates us from God. I also highlight the importance of reading the Bible, as it is the Word of God, and God speaks to us through His Word, the Holy Bible.

During the week, I watched a few talks on YouTube and came across a couple of people from different religious backgrounds being interviewed about their conversion stories to Christianity. Then, the same image I used to describe the white garment I saw at my first healing Mass in our parish appeared on the TV screen (beginning of the book). The husband had seen a similar picture.

On Sunday, 28th April 2024, one of our assistant priests, during his homily, spoke about how it took St Monica 17 years to pray for her son's conversion. Today, he is known as St Augustine, one of the great writers of his era. Many people still quote him today. I have mentioned this in my writings.

6th May 2024: While browsing YouTube, I came across a preacher discussing the importance of dressing modestly when attending church. He speaks of dressing modestly not only at church but at all times. I have included this in my writings.

I was very intrigued by what I was hearing and seeing. It was as though God was trying to send me a message, telling me that he knew everything I had written.

I pray that you have Faith and Believe that what you have read in this book has all been inspired by God the Almighty Father. I have only written what God has permitted me to write and no more.

I believe that with God, nothing is impossible.

May Christ's love, peace, and joy be with you always, and may you be immersed in the aroma of Christ and share it with others.

God Bless you.

THE END

ACKNOWLEDGEMENTS

I want to express my sincere gratitude to Fr. Roni George, VC, for his spiritual guidance and invaluable support throughout the writing of this book, as well as his encouragement during the many times I felt like giving up.

I would also like to thank Fr. Michael Payyapilly, VC, for his support in my spiritual journey, which was crucial in helping me write this book.

I sincerely appreciate and thank Ann Pannaye for agreeing to paint the image for the front cover. It wasn't an easy task, and I'm aware of the challenges she faced during the painting.

Thank you all for your assistance and support.

Endnotes

The Holy Bible -Revised Standard Version- Second Catholic Edition.

Catholic Church. (2000). Catechism of the catholic church (2nd ed.). Our Sunday Visitor.

Augustine, of Hippo, Saint, 354-430. (19401949). The Confessions of Saint Augustine. Mount Vernon: Peter Pauper Press,

Retrieved October 21,2024 from AZQuotes.com Website

Thank You

As we reach the end of this book, I would like to express my gratitude for having taken the time to read it.

I want to disseminate this information to as many people as possible. If you found this book helpful, I would greatly appreciate it if you left me a review. This also helps others find the book.

DISCLAIMER

This memoir is a personal account of my spiritual journey, shared with sincerity and reflection. The experiences, insights, and beliefs expressed are uniquely my own and are not intended to serve as universal truths, professional advice, or religious doctrine. I acknowledge that spirituality is deeply personal, and each individual's path is their own to explore. Readers are encouraged to approach this work with an open heart and mind while drawing their own conclusions. Any interpretations, choices, or actions taken on this memoir are the sole responsibility of the reader. My intention is not to instruct, persuade, or claim absolute truth but simply to share my story in the hope that it may resonate with or inspire others in their own way.

Final Scripture

" Ask, and it will be given you; seek and you will find; knock and it will be opened to you. For everyone who ask receives, and he who seeks finds and to him who knocks it will be opened." (Matthew 7:7)

www.ingramcontent.com/pod-product-compliance
Lightning Source LLC
Chambersburg PA
CBHW060357080526
44583CB00012B/358